THE GREAT SALMON AND SEA TROUT LOUGHS OF IRELAND

The Road to Waterville – MacGillycuddy's Reeks in the background left

Opposite: Furnace – the Millrace butt

THE GREAT
SALMON AND SEA
TROUT LOUGHS
OF IRELAND

Bill Rawlings

SWAN·HILL
PRESS

Author's Note

The scales and the detail in the maps are not meant to be a definitive guide but are an indication only.

Photo credits

The photographs on pages 176, 177, 178, 179 are reproduced by permission of Julyan Rawlings; all other photographs are the copyright of the author.

Copyright © 2002 W. S. B. Rawlings (Text and illustrations)

First published in the UK in 2002 by Swan Hill Press,
an imprint of Quiller Publishing Ltd.

British Library Cataloguing-in-Publication Data
   A catalogue record for this book
   is available from the British Library

ISBN 1 904057 07 1

Typeset by Rowland Phototypesetting Limited,
Bury St Edmunds, Suffolk.
Printed in Italy

Swan Hill Press
an imprint of Quiller Publishing Ltd.
Wykey House, Wykey, Shrewsbury, SY4 1JA, England
Tel: 01939 261616 Fax: 01939 261606
E-mail: info@quillerbooks.com
Website: www.swanhillbooks.com

Contents

	Acknowledgements	6
	Prelude	8
	Foreword by Peter Mantle	10
1	The South-West	11
2	Lough Currane	15
3	Waterville's Upper Lakes	27
4	Lough Caragh and the Glencar System	35
5	River Laune and the Killarney Lakes	43
6	Connemara	51
7	The Ballynahinch System	55
8	Gowla and Others	65
9	Costello and Fermoyle	71
10	The Galway Fishery	81
11	Lough Corrib	87
12	Mayo	97
13	Delphi	99
14	Lough Beltra	113
15	Furnace and Feagh	123
16	Carrowmore	129
17	The Moy System	139
18	The North-West	144
19	Loughs Gill and Glencar	147
20	Lough Melvin and the River Drowse	155
21	Lough Fishing – General Considerations	163
22	Catching Fish	168
23	Western Lough Flies and their Use	174
24	Competitions	183
	Envoi	192
	Appendix: Scottish catch 1900–1990	195
	Recommended Reading	196
	Index	197

Acknowledgements

My ability to write this book reflects my position that shamelessly has involved observation of others – almost in some cases 'poaching' – becoming a bit of a trawler's 'cod-end'. That this started when I was a youth means my thanks are due to a great many people – often now casting their flies elsewhere – for my introduction to the art of lough fishing started some fifty-five years ago.

The contribution to these pages made by staff of the Irish Government has been very considerable, with for the Tourist Board Brian Geraghty in Dublin, and John Lahiffe in London, leading the way. Similarly, in the field, comment by Ken Wheelan at Burrishoole, supported by John Mulrany at Galway, with their ability to open doors on my behalf, gave credibility to my investigations.

Hoteliers who join this supportive party include two generations of the Huggard family at the Butler Arms in Waterville while at Newport Mumford-Smith with Owen beside him, and now Kieran Thompson, have over the years helped me accumulate a great deal of knowledge. To them must be added Patrick O'Flaherty who welcomed me as a new boy to Ballynahinch, as did the team at the Glencar Hotel, and collectively some thirty years of their support has been involved.

At Corrib I was in dire need of informed guidance, obtaining exactly that from John Lanigan-O'Keeffe whose general description of what went on on the lough I badly needed. He introduced me to Frank Costello and Danny MacGoldric who provided plenty of input, and the information that I must visit the Hodsons, who own and run the Carrarevagh Hotel. I did to excellent effect.

Down at Waterville the list of those I need to thank goes back to Jack O'Sullivan – in the early 1970s – the senior member of the family that dominated the boatman's team – and his somewhat wild youngest offspring Tony. Then came a string of other O'Sullivans – Vincent, Brod, Michael to name today's leaders of the clan – making me feel at home the moment I arrive, as do many others who have taken me out on Lough Currane.

Ted O'Riordan, Laune Salmon and Trout Anglers Association, the late Thomas Gallagher on the Drowse, and Terence Bradely at Lough Melvin all gave me on my recent visit their time, and a great deal of information regarding their fisheries that was much needed, while on a previous visit Barry Seagrave did much the same on the fisheries that make up the Moy system.

Seamus Henry has been my mentor for Lough Carrowmore, providing as my boatmen and guides, John Cosgrave, and his son Kenneth, plus Evelyn Cosgrave as a comfortable base from which to operate.

In the past my early talks with Charles Roberts at Furnace – who as inventor of the Bibio must rank high in anyone's batting order – counted for a great deal in my analysis of 'how to' catch sea trout in loughs, while my meeting with Sean Nixon, one of fishing's real champions as guardian of the salmon and white trout that came from the sea into the rivers of Mayo for many years, was a totally unexpected bonus to my research efforts.

Lastly there are my two favourite mini-fisheries, Delphi and Costello, which have been kept going despite the sea lice catastrophe. Many thanks to Peter Mantle, David McEvoy and the others at Delphi where I spent several encouraging days, sea trout numbers rising. The position at Costello is much the same as Geoffrey Fitzjohn and I proved fishing together on Clougher, while his manager Terry Gallaher provided a mass of revealing statistics on how sea trout numbers continue to recover, year after year.

To this list of acknowledgements there remains one name which must be added, that of Peter O'Reilly whose efforts via his books to promote Irish fishing – describing how and where to do it in great detail on both rivers and loughs – has been, for me over the years, of critical importance. As a superb angler himself his opinions are of great interest to fellow fishermen, and for the novice should be noted with great care.

Lastly may I thank Sandy Leventon, editor of *Trout and Salmon*, for permission to use extracts from articles I had written for their excellent publication, which through their monthly reports, covering the whole British Isles, allow us absentees to keep in touch with reality.

Prelude

It is a magic place, the west coast of Ireland. It's where the sun sets and in the old world it inspired men of God to build churches on islands in loughs, to live in beehive cells and give their names to mountains. Here the sea swell comes three thousand miles from Chesapeake Bay, perhaps with a soft warm wind, perhaps on a bad day with sheeting rain and a hurricane. And with that swell the tides bring a silver harvest of fish, the salmon coming three thousand miles too, to find their streams and spawn to maintain the cycle, with beside them their cousins the sea trout. And for the fish the first stop often is a lough close to the ocean, a good place to wait, for many of the river systems are small, draining steep mountains of almost naked rock, unable to hold the moisture, causing instant spates when it rains, the little rivers rising and falling quickly so that with few pools a large fish feels unsafe.

And where the fish are, there will be a man with a rod to catch them when he can. For him in Ireland's far west surrounded by wild mountains and moor, the tang of salt on the air most days, the final triumph that makes the day is a salmon on a fly, with some sea trout for breakfast or maybe a picnic lunch on an island. But just to be there is worth it, to walk the hills a bit and the sands, or have a round of golf, and if it's raining too hard, after lunch one can linger in a bar to get the crack, surprised later at where the time went.

Such is the setting for this book, with the great loughs there in the west – from Kerry in the south to Donegal in the north. Most are close to the sea, some indeed a literal stone's throw away, one we shall visit slightly saline during high tides. Geographically the west coast divides well into four sections, each having a mix of fisheries including a few first class salmon and sea loughs looked at in detail. And set adjacent to the great names are the smaller and less famous trout loughs of the west, covered with reference to their associated rivers. Although this is not a guide book and the majority of detail relates very specifically to the top lough fisheries, a lot of general information on all the waters mentioned has been included to help those new to the region, with a chapter on the particular arts involved when fishing still waters from drifting boats.

Many visiting anglers come already, from England in droves, increasingly from Europe, and some cross the Atlantic, often to visit the land of their ancestors, bringing along a rod. And waiting for them there is every sort of place to stay, from top class hotels, some handsome converted country houses, others purpose built and new, with a mass of cottages to rent, and bed and breakfast lodgings by the hundred. People are relaxed and happy and everywhere you will be made welcome – perhaps surprised to find you like the taste of Irish whiskey and of course Guinness!

To help visiting fishermen the Irish Tourist Board has a comprehensive range of pamphlets, prepared by fishermen for visiting anglers, and kept up to date. This covers in detail the fishings available from top class private river beats to public or free fisheries, while their very detailed guides on all forms of accommodation are remarkable. These can be obtained free through travel agents, who in turn can get them from Dublin or London who will be only too pleased to provide. Meanwhile you can of course approach the Tourist Board direct – also called Bord Failte – at 150 New Bond St, London, W1S 2HQ (020-7518-0800, fax 020-7493-9065) and at Baggot Street Bridge, Dublin 2, Ireland (353 1) 602-4000 and fax 602-4100.

But, the best bit for us fishermen is catching these wild fish from the sea, and if with luck the off-shore drift nets can be removed it may be about to get even better, while learning to catch them, even for experienced anglers used to catching salmon and sea trout in rivers, or reservoir trout with skill, is a genuine challenge.

I hope this book will help the newcomer plan a visit and also give the old hand something to think about. After fifty years of fishing from boats in wild places, I am always learning something new, which is one of the many joys of fishing, and I envy the young angler starting his apprenticeship today.

The wise fisherman new to salmon in loughs will recognise the different elements present and will adapt his approach to fit what he finds, and, when he graduates to become a partner with both place and people, he will have his foot on the bottom rung of a ladder, the top of which few are ever likely to reach.

To complete this book on one of angling's special subjects, I spent six weeks in western Ireland from late July to early September 2001. The purpose was to assemble a large portfolio of photographs, and to visit several fisheries that I did not know that clearly must be included – Lough Melvin and the Drowse River being an excellent example. What I had not expected to find – though I whisper it with fingers and toes crossed – was a sharp improvement in sea trout numbers in systems that until of late had been devastated by the sea lice plague, thanks to the cage rearing of salmon in inshore waters. By feeding the cages with pellets that include a deterrent substance, lice numbers have – in late summer 2001 anyway – been reduced considerably. Thus at Delphi I landed a number of entirely untainted sea trout, going on to Costello to repeat the performance, while at Ballynahinch, and on up the system to Lough Inagh, a remarkable renaissance is taking place. May all our prayers be answered!

The mountains, the fish, the challenge, the loughs and the ocean await us patiently. Good luck to you, and if you can become a partner in this magic place, you will be back time after time.

Foreword by Peter Mantle

Bill Rawlings should be well past his sell-by date. Any normal man of his maturity would have put his feet up a decade ago and settled down to a life of quiet reminiscence in the rose garden. But not Bill.

For Bill, flyfishing is Viagra. Long after his battery was meant to have worn out, he continues to tear about like a teenager newly released from confinement. His extraordinary enthusiasm, his limitless energy and his lively mind offer hope of perpetual excitement to those of us now ploughing through the middle age doldrums.

In this wonderfully optimistic book Bill has managed to combine his vast experience of flyfishing with romance, practicality, provocation and an almost youthful curiosity. While I might baulk at some of his conclusions, or quibble with the occasional description, he has also managed to remind me of just what it was that drew me to Ireland – the sumptuous scenery, the glowing generosity of spirit, the wit and, of course, the incredible variety of fishing.

I have not fished even half the lakes described by Bill. But he has surely made me want to plug all the many gaps in my Irish piscatorial CV. And I can now do so with a major addition to my armoury.

So many fishing books are long on dogma and short on colour – turgid litanies of fish caught, lifeless technical tips or hackneyed anecdotes. This one is different. To wield a cliché, Bill's opus simply gladdens the heart and fills the mind.

The devastation of many west of Ireland lakes by the monstrous new salmon farms looks depressingly likely to continue apace. Several of Bill's chosen fancies are, sadly, pale shadows of their former selves. He is kind to them. If nothing else, this book should nourish a new enthusiasm for preserving these gems from man's stupidity. For without its glorious lake fishing, Ireland would be hugely diminished.

Peter Mantle,
Delphi,
July 2002

Chapter 1
The South-West

Ireland is shaped like a soup plate, being mainly flat and low in the centre, with hills and mountains round the outside. Nowhere is this more true than in the south-west where the massive range of MacGillycuddy's Reeks, including Ireland's highest mountain, Carrantoohill, at 3414ft (1040m) is the water source for three famous salmon river systems. The remoteness of these high hills is also remarkable, for a wartime crashed bomber was only discovered fifty years after its loss.

The three river systems include to the east, and made famous by Bing Crosby, the Killarney lakes and River Laune – the next west is the Caragh, or Glencar, system draining into Dingle Bay, backdrop to the film *Ryan's Daughter* – followed by literally at the end of the (once railway) line, famous Lough Currane at Waterville, with its hill loughs behind arguably the best sea trout and salmon lake fishery left in the British Isles today. From there, west over Ballinskellig Bay upon whose shingle bank Waterville is built, head on out to sea past the holy rocks of the Skellig Islands with their monks' beehive stone cells, and next stop is Boston, Mass.!

Like other south-western peninsulas in these Islands, several in Scotland, but typically Cornwall, and Pembroke, both the place and the people of Kerry have retained a special and personal individuality. By nature they are different, almost another race, possibly because since they are not on the way to anywhere locals did not get the chance to cross-breed, the reverse of those within cities, or central regions that are criss-crossed by road arteries and their itinerant populations. In County Kerry – and Norfolk is similar – you therefore will find Kerrymen who, while in Ireland, are not typical Irishmen, just as Cornishmen are a long way from being typical Englishmen.

Kerry also seems to have an almost classless society, one where rich and poor, British, French and American anglers are welcomed happily from the heart. If anyone were to put their nose in the air they would not enjoy themselves for long – and they would not begin to understand what they were missing. If you are unable to have, maybe, a drink or two too many with your boatman after a great day on Currane, and take part in a bit of a leg-pull on how you did it – what flies and how – then you won't be comfortable in the bars of Waterville. But most of us fit well – dukes or dustmen – and most of us who have done just that know we will be returning when we can, drawn by the lake and its fish, the skills needed for a renewed challenge, and the locals who go on being themselves faithful friends for life!

Waterville was not the first place that I went fishing in Ireland. That was Newport, in

Mayo, in July 1969, fishing Lough Beltra and the Burrishoole system, prime target the sea trout, and based at the glorious Georgian Newport House Hotel. But my next visit two years later was to the south-west, flying to Cork and hiring a car, driving west up the Lee valley on the Killarney road, turning left down to Kenmare. There I joined the famous Ring of Kerry, the circular trip from Killarney for sixty miles with the mountains inland, and the sea on the other hand. From Kenmare, after crossing the prolific little Blackwater River, then through Sneam, it was twenty-five miles to Waterville, where the first feature before the town is the bridge above the remarkable Butlers Pool, just yards from the tide and of course I stopped to have a look. From the sea to Lough Currane is about two hundred yards, and I could see a number of boats out fishing – in late July both for trout and salmon.

I was booked in at the Butler Arms Hotel – another perfect fisherman's base – and enquired how I should set about going fishing for the next two weeks. The management were a help, but it was high season, and to find a good boatman would not be so easy – something I discussed with another Englishman, in the bar before dinner, who was leaving the next day. He asked if I would like to take on his man.

Despite the warning that he was 'rather a wild lad', I agreed to meet Tony O'Sullivan next morning in the car park at nine o'clock. He made it by 9.45 – mid twenties, unshaven, with a terrible hangover – believing, I discovered later, that I had never fished before. We duly set forth in his boat which was largely held together by paint. Despite my protests we were trolling spinners behind the outboard, and half an hour later a salmon took solidly, fifty yards off the shore past the entry bay for the Cummeragh River. Having exchanged a string of four letter words regarding how I should play the fish, he became aware that, contrary to his belief that I had never fished before, I had been fishing since before he was born and that I did not need to be told by him how to land a salmon!

With the fish in the net – the flask a salute – thereafter we fished a fly and each had a couple of trout of between 2lb and 3½lb to lay out with the salmon on a tray in the hotel's hall, alongside others.

The names given to sea trout in these islands are numerous, with the most common in Ireland in those days, descriptively, white trout. This was and is further reduced in the west to just trout, possibly because they outnumber their brown cousins, although today sea trout in full has become common. With salmon, grilse in Ireland's west are called peel, which in Devon and Cornwall means sea trout. It keeps you on your toes!

My son Julyan and I became good friends with Tony, as we have with many of the O'Sullivans, having great days together, picking up a lot on how to catch Irish salmon and sea trout, in lakes. Then sadly I heard he had drowned a few years back in an accident – of course in the lake.

That, therefore, is a sketched outline of how I started on a love affair with the far south-west, drawn to it much as were those holy men a thousand years and more ago. Boston continues to move away from Waterville at the speed your finger nails grow, so who knows when that great edge off which man may fall will reappear. And who knows what may happen if over the next five years the stranglehold of the Irish drift nets is removed – their take in the year 2000 being 71.3 per cent of the total Irish salmon catch and the long term average being about 80 per cent. Because the nets are located mainly off the west, and north-west coasts, it is clear that the immediate beneficiaries from such a removal would be those salmon fisheries adjacent to their operating areas although a great many will have been heading for the English Channel's rivers as well as including the salmon fisheries of France, Spain and Portugal.

Just what impact this would have on Currane's annual salmon take of some four hundred is speculation but it has to be very considerable. What is more the huge increase in the numbers of fish spawning which would follow, must lead to a reversal of the fifty year trend of falling stock numbers, as the grotesque netting take of around 160,000 salmon and grilse would cease! The fishing is a lot of fun today, but just think what it might become in say 2010!

Meanwhile on the Waterville system, the white trout fishing, not long ago hit hard by sea lice problems emanating from the salmon farms up the coast, has made a great recovery. The big fellows are back from April onwards with their younger cousins following in increasing numbers as the days lengthen. There are no members of the salmon family that I know of which will test your skills more surely than the sea trout, whose power and speed is truly remarkable.

We will now look at the three systems in the south-west in detail, examining what to expect at which times of year, and how to catch fish! It is opening day, 17 January, on Currane, plenty of fish have been seen, it is cold with a lot of snow on the tops, but the gentle breeze from the west is what we want – even a fly might do it!

The boat slips quietly out of the little harbour, it is half past nine, there are several others ahead, the Cummeragh river bay occupied since dawn.

The new season has started.

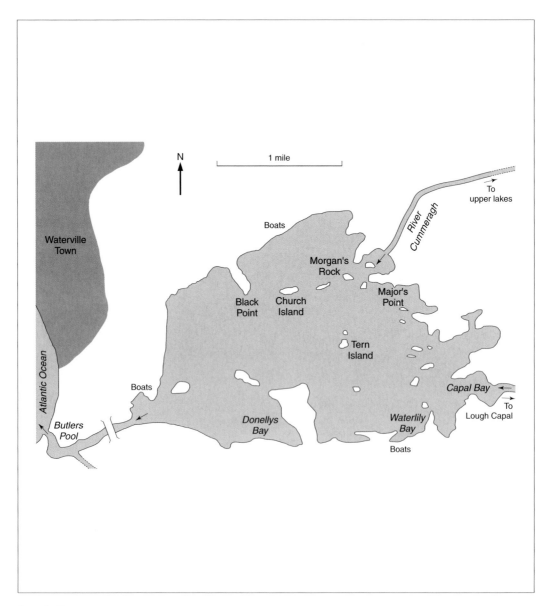

Lough Currane

Chapter 2
Lough Currane

Unless he has his own helicopter, when the last thirty miles on a clear day will be breathtaking, the fisherman's anticipation on the road to Waterville, by whatever route he takes, will stir the nearer he gets. And when round a corner he suddenly is there, with the lake and the town, and the sea immediately before him, exactly as with the Corrib or Loch Maree, he will know instantly that here is a great lake fishery. This is a fisherman's Mecca, and as with most fisheries of unique standing many of the great names of the past went there. Indeed, in his book *The Salmon*, in the 'Fur Feather and Fin' series of sporting books, published in 1898 by Longmans Green, the Hon. A.E. Gaythorne-Hardy, selects Waterville and Lough Currane above all others to illustrate what lake fishing for salmon is all about. Discarding Loch Tay, he wrote that 'fishing there is best in the spring, and it must be desperately cold work trailing the big phantom minnows after your boat in a north-east wind'. Clearly he liked to fish a fly whenever he could so he suggests his readers should note his good days in a certain 'damp climate contiguous to a melancholy ocean', with his 'testimony to the excellence of the free fishing at Waterville', in the 1860s.

It is fascinating reading, with comments on the size of the boat required to deal with 'the violent squalls and heavy storms', that 'the favourite fly was a moderate sized sea trout fly, with a rough body of fiery brown pig's wool'. The fishing method 'was like that for ordinary loch trout,' by 'drifting sideways along the likely bays and headlands, casting before you with the wind with a fourteen-foot rod and a moderate line'. The sea trout were 'almost anywhere', while the 'salmon had favourite haunts and lurking places where submerged rocks rose nearly to the surface in deep water. There was of course some competition to secure the first turn at the favourite places' and rivalry between boatmen over who could get the best baskets of fish!

Their two boatmen were 'full of stories', they organised picnics on islands where they broiled sea trout in the embers of a fire 'as a pièce de résistance', and were noticeably keen on the whiskey. They also allowed themselves for 'the best day we ever had there' to be 'bribed and cajoled' into fishing in a full gale when not one other boat set forth. It started well 'and before we had finished the drift we had secured over two dozen sea trout, a big brown fish [salmon], and four peel [grilse]' before disaster struck, when an oar broke and the boat nearly capsized, half filling with water! They managed to beach the craft and had a long wet walk home.

Much of which sounds largely very similar to today, although it is outboards and not oars that matter, which these days very seldom break down. Which said the number of fish they landed in a single unfinished drift is astonishing – even if it had nearly involved the length of the lake, in westerly gale conditions that can be excellent for catching fish.

Another old angler, to become famous in his day, was Walter Barrett who caught his first salmon trailing a spoon on Currane in 1911, later to be a great taker of salmon on the Wye with four of over 40lb. Elsewhere, on the Kennet he invented the Shaving Brush, and Hatching Nymph Mayflies, then went to Sweden where he 'discovered' the Em River, holding for many years the world sea trout record at 26½lb.

Exactly how the quite small Waterville system produced in those days such huge numbers of fish – against today's not unreasonable catch – from spawning beds that have not shrunk in size, is inexplicable, and why should this not be achieved today, with a little help from man?

What one might call the Currane watershed is curiously small, being about half that of its immediate, very close neighbour the River Inny which drains some forty-seven

South shore Currane in the evening

square miles. There is however a huge difference in the land drained, with the Inny a broad fertile valley running ten miles inland, fed regularly by tributaries from the hills that follow parallel at each side, at the far end Mount Colly being 2258ft (823m). It is an excellent little spate river where in good water after rain you can just about guarantee a grilse or fresh salmon in the summer and autumn. There are also plenty of sea trout, which makes a day on the river an excellent alternative to non-stop boating. For what it is worth, and one should not ignore the likes of Noel Huggard – one of Ireland's greatest hoteliers ever (sometime owner and manager of Ballynahinch, Ashford Castle, and of course the Butler Arms hotels) and a first class angler – salmon in the River Inny have a particular preference for flies that are pale in colour, with plenty of yellow as a feature up to size 6. It's certainly worked for me, while in high water a light two inch Yellow Belly Devon spinner has also done the trick.

But the lakes are fed by the big mountains, huge masses of rock starting just south of Currane and running east, nothing flat and fertile here, a home for ravens and once eagles, steep cliffs and deep gorges, a few sheep, and that's it. As one would expect the land's ability to hold water is almost nil, a few small rocky hollows having ponds and marshy bogs, drained by streams into a series of upper lakes – some within the scope of migratory fish. Thence, their outflows concentrate into the Cummeragh River, being with one small exception – the Capal stream in the south-east corner – the only river entering Currane, thereafter to reach the Atlantic via that famous Butlers Pool. Through this bottleneck thousands of smolts migrate each year while, starting in the frosts of January with snow on the mountains, the first springers nose back in on a high tide, followed for the next nine months by summer salmon and grilse. A mass of sea trout follow, with the big ones, averaging 4 to 8lb first in April and May, becoming smaller progressively, although the 'juniors' of August at Currane will mostly make about 1lb in weight.

Spring salmon will average at least 10lb in most years, while the grilse run at 5 to 6lb. Given reasonable conditions there is hardly a day in the year when you will not have a chance with a fly, provided you know where to go, and being a big shallow lake there are plenty of lies to try, often the same old 'lurking places' that never change. Certainly in a freezing north wind in February to trail a big Toby, or as we used to do a silver sprat, at a gentle pace behind a modern outboard will be the best option in the circumstances, which we all would agree does not mean much contribution from the angler – unless he is driving the boat himself. However I have loved mackerel fishing all my life, and surely this is the peak of that activity, while if you like messing about in boats, and starting a fire on a headland sheltered behind some rocks to get the kettle going, with a dram of anti-freeze slipping down well, you won't be disappointed with the company you find there to warm your soul, as the gulls line up in certain expectation!

And as the last boat joins us on the island, when you set eyes on the glorious, silver and lilac 14lb springer that Brod O'Sullivan holds up, taken a few minutes ago, sure it's his brother we'll be netting ourselves later on, even if it's now snowing a bit.

The fishing on Currane remains free to this day, and while a highly experienced lough fisherman would do quite well with the trout, and be able to catch a few salmon on his own, that same angler would be the first to admit how much better he would do with one of the expert local boatmen at the oars. Certainly the obvious areas to concentrate one's efforts are the same with most salmon lake fisheries, so that on Currane the mouths of the Cummeragh, and to a lesser extent the smaller Capal, rivers make very visible targets. However it is far from obvious that Morgan's Rock, or the Major's Point, should be superior to any number of similar features, at the eastern end of the lough.

While the white trout are very much more widely spread all over Currane, having an expert local with you is a huge advantage on your first visit, to fish the best salmon lies correctly. It is also a lot of fun when you want to catch up with events, or hear which flies are doing the damage. At the same time, as discussed in the subsequent chapter on tactics, to fish the salmon lies correctly calls for proper boat control.

Currane is big and open

Ballinskellig Bay

So it was for myself on my first spring visit at the end of March 1972, fishing with Vincent O'Sullivan who had just returned to become a full time boatman, and for a long time has remained a leading light of the fishing world in Waterville. I only had two days, having spent some time on the Blackwater on my way, a brief trip with children – aged from fourteen to nineteen – before going to work abroad.

Day one was windless – which meant trolling – as was the next morning, but a modest breeze from the south-west arrived in the afternoon so up went the fly rod. With Vincent easing the boat gently down on to Morgan's Rock I got one beauty of 12lb, and failed to hook two others that came at the fly, probably through striking too fast – the sea trout angler's usual problem when after the slow taking salmon. These fish were within a few yards of the rocks, total area involved about fifty yards by twenty-five, following the south side of the little island. On tactics, with much more later, I should mention the successful fly had been tied by Vincent the night before – under instruction from Jack O'Sullivan the doyen of the clan, being size 4 and on the tail, with a size 6 Hairy Mary on the bob. Its pattern came from no book and some years later I described it in an article as 'a gaudy fly with a red hackle and perhaps sheep's wool in its body, a silver tinsel rib, and a mallard or teal wing. Tied on a single hook, in my ignorance it looked fine to me for a Waterville fish, and the conditions were improving all the time'. However, I cannot imagine either Vincent or me picking such a curious creation today, the Hairy Mary by all means, but with a Silver Stoat or a large Black Pennel, far more likely and very possibly no larger than a size 8 double at that. But handsome is as handsome does!

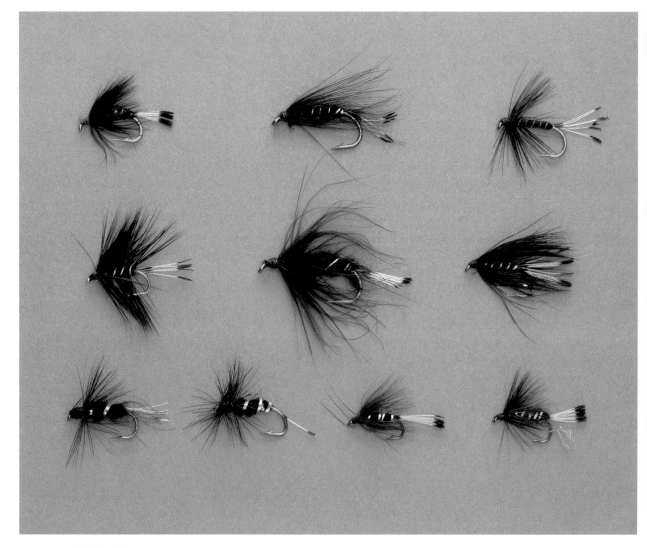

All Black Pennels

Then it gets warmer and the fish wake up, grilse averaging over 5lb arriving on most tides, with ever-increasing numbers of smaller sea trout in the 2 to 4lb range. And while the regular salmon lies remain well stocked, with increasing numbers in the lake your chance of a fish from other rocks and points improves too. Ordinary quite small sea trout flies, lighter tackle and single handed rods take over, and with the long days, while very few people fish on late, one could keep going to midnight. They say night fishing for the white trout doesn't work, but it gives the place a well earned rest – and, as another good cause, helps the bar profits!

In chapter 21 I deal with the equipment which one requires in detail, suffice to say here that over the season you need to be prepared for trolling heavy and light baits, and for fishing floating and sinking lines with double and single handed rods. When fishing with a boatman, he will bring the trolling rods, net and outboard, but in all events be careful to check who is responsible for what.

One of the best day's fishing that I have ever had anywhere was during my first visit to Waterville with my younger son Julyan. We had picked up a lot from Tony and found ourselves having more trout to show for our efforts than the others on most days.

Mid second week it rained a bit harder at night (actually it rained almost every night) and I woke to see the last of heavy clouds lifting and moving east, inland, leaving a balmy wet trail behind them. Thinking of a salmon, I was up early to have a look at the Inny, the local river that I mentioned as independent of the Currane system. I found it, I thought, relatively low but falling, and I put a stick in the beach by the bridge, returning for breakfast, and booking the bottom beat before anyone else could. The plan therefore was to have a go at the river and forget the lough, since with falling water conditions the river should be perfect.

Armed for salmon, and back at my marker, the level had changed not one inch since before breakfast -–curious! However I went to the top of the beat with spinning rod only, and Julyan fished the lower water with Tony. I had got it wrong – the river had not moved because the full weight of the rain had not in fact reached the hills until I was back having breakfast. Thus what happened next was that between about 10 am and midday the river rose ten inches! Despite this, I landed one salmon of 8lb on a Kerryman spoon, and lost another of similar size thanks to a spring in my fixed-spool reel breaking. Have you ever tried playing a lively fish with a broken reel and thirty yards of line out – very difficult. Meanwhile Julyan caught a sea trout of 1½lb, and we met for a conference. The river was still rising and we decided to go back to Currane for an early lunch and the afternoon afloat in an increasing south-west wind. How right we were!

We had a quick picnic by the boats – volcano kettle tea of course, which is obligatory – launched and headed south-west to the far side of the lake, not too distant from the other hotel – the Waterville Lake. Daddies were being blown over the water in the warmth of the rising south-west wind and it was firm and steady but no gale. Sea trout were showing everywhere, and the first in the boat took my artificial Daddy fished on the bob – this one right on the surface.

This success by the Daddy was however the exception, since all the other fish taken that afternoon fell to identical size 10 Black Pennels. Now this is a fly which comes in many shapes and sizes that vary from almost a nymph body with a spider hackle, to a heavily palmered style which is almost a Zulu with a tippet tail. The body material varies from flat floss to woolly seal's fur, the rib from the finest wire to broad silver tinsel, while hackles can be long or short. You can fish three Black Pennels on a cast and offer an attractive variation of lure – and indeed I have tried it to good effect. At Tony's insistence our version that day was woolly seal's fur, broad tinsel, and fairly well palmered, to this day in my view a perfect lough fly.

We drifted a long sweep, missing the west end of Church Island, with Tony fishing an experimental rod I had had made by Ogden Smith. It was a single handed, soft 12ft, two piece, fibre glass rod. It was far too floppy for me and I gave it to Tony who felt it would be just the thing for the 'wallopers' – his name for the big sea trout. And sure enough during our drift one of these jumped several times a long way in front of us, right off the point of Church Island, while Tony swore he would get him. He did – 6½lb of quite fresh trout (walloper, sea trout, white trout) to add to our growing harvest. And it went on, during that afternoon we netted twelve sea trout shared equally, with an average weight rather over 3lb! The decision to leave the river had been correct, and conditions had gone our way – but we had had the sense to change horses ourselves.

We returned to the back bar at the hotel to celebrate, handing over the fish to be laid out in the hall for all to see! There strangely, as things had gone so well, we were about the first back to the hotel, and together with Tony took up position, with our backs to the wall, in the corner by the window. (The bar itself was an island, roughly square with the populace able to surround the one barman, and barmaid, landlocked in the centre.) Pints of the black stuff – chilled or not, described as 'a hot one, or a cold one' came forth and fellow anglers trickled in from their cars. A rotten day they said, totally dead in the morning, and coming short after lunch. We kept our mouths shut – not a hint would we give – but we knew sooner or later truth would out.

Then big Michael Morriarty went next door, down the passage to the office in the hotel hall, to get a message – and came back with the news!

'Did you see that plate of fish?'

A number of rather tired heads lifted – what fish was that then?

'A salmon and thirteen trout with two near the size of a salmon!'

There was a scramble – and why not – and they all came back wanting to know how, with what fly, where on the lough and when. And indeed since the best return by any other boat had been four, with most having only two or three modest sized sea trout to lay out, what on earth had we been up to – and do have another Bushmills!

The truth of course was that in no way had we done anything out of the ordinary.

A Waterville regular – Charlie Chaplin

Tony had taken four fish with the largest 6½lb – I had netted one of over 5lb – and the remainder between us had been not smaller than 2lb. Total weight had been 39lb for the afternoon with an 8lb salmon and one more sea trout from the morning. It took two trays to carry the display and the pressure on their captors was ferocious – how did we do it?

Being generous by nature, I started to tell the then admiring audience the truth – that in fact eleven of the twelve had taken a choice Black Pennel, when I received on my right ankle a sharp kick from Tony. He took over.

Never, he said, saw you such a fly – and unless, he stated, we had a master fly tier here never might we play such a trick on the fish again. For only once did he see that fly – and two flies only had we until one was snapped away in that devil of a flyer – and the other was in the end chewed to bits by the last one we had in the boat, so we came home.

Ah! But the fly itself? They demanded to know!

It was strange, and it overall looked almost a black grey – but it had orange in the body with a touch of green in the hackle that was otherwise mainly mallard wing, and the tail was tippet. Sure you never saw a fly like it!

Half a mile of mombretia

I withdrew to have a bath, a celebratory dinner, and to accept with modesty the continuing accolades that the angling residents – most of the hotel – continued to thrust towards us, together with further inquiry regarding the miracle fly, its style of employment and the location of our best fish. As this research was not untypically linked to the arrival of yet another round of large Bushmills and Guinness, which taught Julyan a useful lesson to boot, I in the end made a far from steady lurch for the stairs to bed. I did not, either, feel inspired to nip down to the Inny to view the early prospects the following morning!

A leisurely breakfast led to a relatively silent two mile journey to the boats, and we arrived last of the whole team. Here we found that not one of them was going to set forth until our very expert advice had been taken concerning the contents of their fly boxes. Yes we said – quite like that – no we said nothing like this one – but we said why not try a size 10 Black Pennel, tied with black seal's fur, well picked out, wide tinsel ribbing, and a palmered hackle?

We ourselves went on using the latter, and thanks to Tony seemed to come home with more than most of them. But never again did we then, or later, or elsewhere, capture in one day mainly from a lake about 50lb weight of very edible fish – one salmon and thirteen sea trout.

County Kerry was exceptionally dry in 2001, with minimal rainfall after April, until just before I arrived in late August when a few days of heavy rain did occur with a short spate drawing a lot of fish out of Currane into the upper lakes. Thereafter it was a heatwave, hopeless for the lake, with even the Butlers Pool failing to produce – although not short of fish. I tried hard myself, the first time I had ever fished it, with Vincent and Michael O'Sullivan, and Geoffrey Gardine, Charlie Chaplin's grandson aged fifteen, being a prodigy of Vincent's and good for his age. In fact Chaplin was a great lover of Waterville and for many years a regular visitor, his statue, in classic movie attire, is on the front beside the sea.

Excellent and reasonably priced food was available in the Lobster Bar – where one night I was up until 2 am – and which has become the nerve centre for fishing at Waterville.

The famous Butlers Pool – Michael O'Sullivan fishing

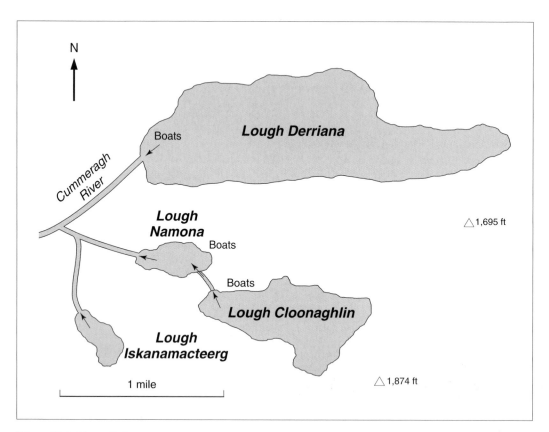

Waterville's Upper Lakes

Chapter 3

Waterville's Upper Lake

There are four fishable lakes in the upper reaches of the Cummeragh River system. All are above the 500ft (152m) contour, spectacularly placed, and in my view remarkably under-fished. Today they are owned by a new group, who also purchased the Lobster Bar from Michael O'Sullivan, the idea being to develop the lakes' considerable potential, as in the past their employment was limited to visitors having an odd day – say one in a fortnight's visit for a change. All the Currane boatmen know their way round the top lakes, but they all prefer their regular waters given the option, and are far from being great experts.

Namona – home of big sea trout. Cloonaghlin is on the left.

Down below, feeding into the south-east corner of Currane, the Capal River drains the Isknagahiny (also Capal) Lough as a much smaller contributor, having excellent spawning streams feeding the little system, and a reputation for producing big sea trout late in the season. It can, as I once discovered, suffer curious wind effects in half a south-west gale, something that is due entirely to the proximity of the adjacent range of hills, running up to 1786ft (544m), immediately to the south. Nothing in my view is more irritating than a constantly changing wind direction, or makes good fishing technique almost impossible, and what is more I believe it disturbs the trout equally! That said, I also believe that on a quiet and warm September evening, not long after some rain, that by fishing with great caution into the dark, this lough could produce an astonishing basket of fish. Not salmon, as it doesn't feel like a serious salmon fishery, but big, and very big white trout.

Back up the hill, via the Cummeragh river which has a number of attractive stretches that fish well – and not ignoring the slow canal-like bits in a good wind – I believe that exactly the same can be said about Lough Namona which is a very similar size, having also a reputation for particularly large trout. It is more or less a resting place below Lough Cloonaghlin, a short distance up over the heather, its connecting stream, where it flows into the lake, providing a superb lie, fishable from both a boat and the bank. Here when ashore, at all costs keep well away from the water, and the very obvious attractions that the current inflow offers, even to the extent of crawling along the shore. Similarly when boating keep all of 20 yards (18m) out of it, with not a wave that shouldn't be there or particularly any raps on the boat's hull! Stalked like this in high season, without bright sun on the water, if you will place your flies softly just beyond the stream's movement – starting only a few feet from the bank – you will have a great chance. Here you probably will get a fair sized trout, but once I hooked in September something much larger, that let go after ten minutes, and never one broke the surface. With a single-handed rod I could do nothing but – being on the bank – follow as the fish moved first to my right and then to my left, taking with him all my line and about 100 yards of backing. From experience I think he was at least 15lb, and because of his stately perambulations a salmon and not a trout – and it could have been hooked in the back too. I think he was on the tail fly which was, improbably for me, a Peter Ross size 8. To which I must add this comment, which is that I wanted a fairly heavy fly on the tail, and a quick sinker, to balance the leader – the bob being a Bibio, and the dropper a Black Pennel, both size 10. Those who have fished a lot will get my point about the balance, while similarly those who have fished high in the hills for salmon will know the silver flashiness of a Peter Ross in moving water is likely to deliver the goods. Down at sea level at Currane I would not even consider this famous old Loch Tay stalwart – but there is a time and place for us all!

Namona is a shallow lough and the whole of it can be fished for both white trout and salmon, but if it is salmon you want, go for the point of inflow – where I hooked my fish.

Derriana – the north shore in August

Derriana – the outflow and boats

Immediately above Namona is Cloonaghlin Lough which is hardly fished, but in my view should be, albeit a lot of it is deep and not easy fishing. But the simple truth is that, and the same applies to Lough Iskanamacteerg on a parallel tributary from the Cummeragh River half a mile over the hill, nobody seems to know much about these waters, or indeed how to fish them.

Maybe this makes them excellent reservoirs for fish as well as water, and perhaps that is how they should be left. But I am quite sure that plenty of both salmon and white trout climb the hillsides to get to these remote loughs each year, and I know that their location in the mountains is genuinely unique, while terribly vulnerable to bad weather, with many days impossible.

And just as special is Lough Derriana which is the best of them all. Here is a lake that from the west is wide open to the visiting angler as he comes to load and launch his boat and becomes almost a gorge as it runs away east into the arms of

Knocknagantee at 2220ft (670m), while leaning over the water to the south is a further 1700ft (518m) of close escarpment. They say salmon in numbers are here in January on opening day, but they say too then it is a brave man – or an idiot – who would go afloat on the lake until April when the storms have gone. And from personal experience I can confirm the danger for I once saw Derriana at its worst in late September when in a force 8 gale I fished it with Tom Corchoran – an expedition stimulated by the fact he had to return to Dublin the next day, and had booked the boat, having also a brand new and excellent electric start outboard! I have been in typhoons in Hong Kong and Japan, I have been at sea in a force 10 gale, but the awesome prospect that faced us was truly remarkable, which I described at the time as follows:

> We parked the car by the boats, which had been pulled far up the beach and turned over for protection, and looked aghast at the turmoil. The far end of the

Cummeragh River – just below Derriana

lough, the 'finger', was blotted out by a solid sheet of white, a cross between cloud, rain, and water, from which emerged, from time to time, white twisting columns that moved menacingly across the lough. At the point where these 'spouts' met the surface, the water was churned into a mass of agitated small waves, white like the white of an egg in a mixer bowl.

A quite small 'spout' which looked harmless enough came through the boat while we were fishing, being far more destructive than we had thought possible, requiring urgent action to grab anything loose – fly boxes etc – before they took off!

That day a big heavily dressed size 8 Zulu accounted for six big trout from 2 to 4¾lb in weight, while a Blue Zulu that Tom had on the bob was blown – before our very eyes – out of the mouth of a grilse that had gone for it. I have caught salmon much higher up in Glen Feshie at the top of the Spey, but nowhere that I know can compare with Derriana as a mountain lake fishery, where salmon and sea trout can be taken consistently in decent numbers. Add to that its remarkable location, the clarity of its water, which holds also quite takeable brown trout, and you will see why I place Derriana on such a remarkable pedestal. It is very far from easy fishing, but with skill and, as we showed, fortitude, the scope is huge. But above all you must have a solid boat, a good engine, and take the greatest care, since I have no doubt that one of the big water spouts would have sunk us.

From limited experience, and advice from others who know the lough, the open and quite shallow western bays hold white trout, as does the long stretch of the north rocky shore, being typical and classic salmon water – very close in, right in the jumble of waves and foam. But, as we found on that wild day, while the lee shore fished well, the moment you were into a fish you needed to get out in the lake at once, or risk shipwreck. In truth we would have done better, without a boatman to fish Hebridean style, taking it in turns to fish, one of us at the oars holding the boat head to wind, thirty yards off, edging progressively and slowly crabwise to cover the lies fully. As it was, by going out 150 yards to drift back in worked, more or less, thanks to Tom's excellent new outboard.

This remarkable day on Derriana took place almost thirty years ago, and we only managed about three hours actual fishing, but I can remember it in every detail as though it was yesterday. I have never before been so wet, or enjoyed what was in fact quite a major triumph, for we were the only boat to be launched that day at Waterville, and we came back rewarded, our hero the size 8 Zulu taking all six trout! No other fly caught a thing, and I believe that something even larger could have worked in the foam of the lee shore's rocks.

The lake itself has excellent grazing on its northern side, the fields bright green with lush grass, a vivid contrast to the dull browns of the peaty mountain sides. The lough's water is also particularly clear which is a feature typical of mountain lakes, Doo Lough at Delphi being an excellent example. To spend a season or two studying Waterville's upper lakes in detail, and Derriana in particular I believe might surprise some old angling regulars! With the geology a long way from pure acid peat bog, this may be the key to the Currane system's prolific output, and the answer to my earlier question on how so small a river system could provide such huge numbers of fish. There has to be a logical solution, and rich headwater conditions, good for raising juvenile salmonids, fits the bill.

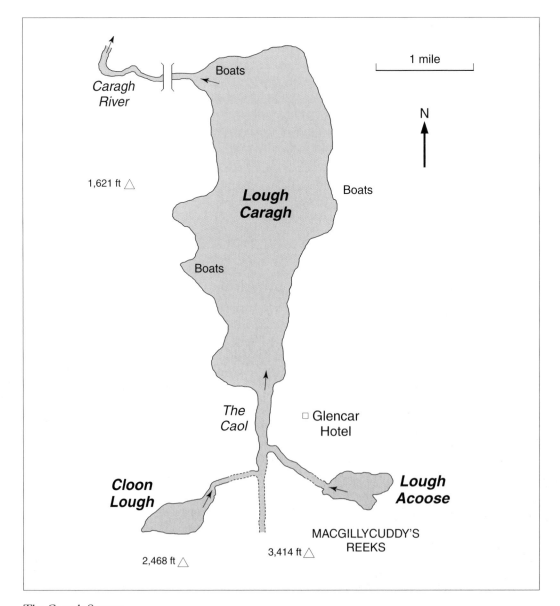

Caragh River

Boats

1 mile

1,621 ft △

Boats

Lough Caragh

Boats

The Caol

☐ Glencar Hotel

N

Cloon Lough

Lough Acoose

MACGILLYCUDDY'S REEKS

2,468 ft △

3,414 ft △

The Caragh System

Chapter 4

Lough Caragh and the Glencar System

I mentioned the Ring of Kerry as a glorious trip in your car, but for an even more spectacular drive go from Waterville to the Glencar Hotel by the direct route, via the Inny valley and over a pass from which the view is breathtaking. The road becomes steeper and steeper as you emerge from a considerable area of forest – which includes hardwoods – with at the brow a sharp ridge, falling almost as a cliff from below your feet, and a huge bowl of country stretching right on to the massive line of peaks known as MacGillicuddy's Reeks. If you don't want to stop to take it all in you must be an odd character – or in a great hurry – but what you see, so spread out for thirty miles looking north-east, is the Caragh system's catchment area, the hills that draw to them the rain clouds in particular.

The Caragh River just above the lough

The Glencar Hotel is the traditional base for anglers, owning as it does the fishing above Lough Caragh on both the river and hill loughs. Below the lough the river is in the hands of a local company which issues permits to visitors. The lough itself can be fished by hiring a boat, with or without a boatman, from one of a number of sources, and local enquiry will put you in touch with those involved.

The great feature of the system is the continuing excellence of its run of spring salmon, and it is as a salmon river rather than a sea trout river that it should be considered, although the lower river in particular can produce numbers of rather small sea trout in late summer.

'Where the spawners go'

Lough Cloon – deep in the hills.

In addition the upper lakes, Acoose, Cloon, and Reagh have salmon from the spring onwards, while the best fishing is after a good summer flood that brings the grilse up in numbers. These high loughs are, like Derriana, vulnerable to rapid changes in weather, but being right under the Reeks their beauty is remarkable. At the same time there are a lot of brown trout present which means for the fly fisherman, in the right conditions, plenty of action – even if their size is largely small.

This brings me to the subject of fishing methods employed on the system, almost from top to bottom. Except for sea trout fishing on the lower river for which the fly is popular, almost everywhere else its use today has been abandoned: on Lough Caragh and even the small upper lakes, trolling with an outboard is the universal method used. Similarly on the Glencar Hotel water, much of it ideal for the fly which once was the normal way of catching fish, the spinner, and bait is now in charge. Why this should be so is to me inexplicable, not least when at Waterville, a few miles away the reverse is the case! With the sort of glorious, very well maintained, fly water the hotel has available, to see a non-stop barrage of heavy metal, and worms, makes one weep – it never was the tradition, and it need not be now.

The Caragh River in spate

For Lough Caragh to be treated in the same way – although everywhere it is more traditional to troll for early springers – is completely unnecessary since, exactly as one finds with all lakes, there are always salmon lies to be tried wherever you are. Indeed on Acoose where I had one day on my visit recently, I rose what I am sure were two grilse, and saw three salmon show, close to the shore near where the boats are kept, and at the mouth of the incoming river. It was a cloudless day with little wind, making fishing difficult, although I did net twenty-four brown trout up to 1¼lb, a daddy on the bob doing the damage. This lough, together with Cloon which I had a good look at but didn't fish, have I am sure great potential for a proficient lough angler and should warrant a serious effort.

The hotel beats take an average of 250 to 350 salmon a year, while the score for Lough Caragh seems to be a bit of a mystery. The same goes for the lower river

High up the Caragh

which in the right water, and everyone I spoke to agreed, could produce very big bags indeed. My guess is that the two together are likely to equal the upper river, and there certainly should not be the large number of boats in use if it wasn't worthwhile.

My day on the Glencar River, on the bottom beat immediately above Lough Caragh, looked to me to have great promise, there having been heavy rain two days before so that the river was high and falling – coloured, but not bad. Vincent, the head gillie came with me and fished hard with my spinning rod while I worked away with a fly. Fish were showing all over the place, good sized salmon as well as grilse, and to hook one – or even half a dozen – seemed to be a certainty! But we moved nothing, nor did others fishing above us, all legal means having been tried, a highly improbable outcome, and due I am sure to the fact that the spate was the first for so long, making a dash for the upper river their sole concern.

Caragh headwaters – Lough Acoose

I have seen this refusal to look at spinner or fly by a lot of fish before, in exactly the same circumstances. In the mid-1980s, on the Ullapool river at the falls pool I could sit on a rock, with salmon and grilse touching my feet, being completely ignored. In much the same way, one presumes that in western America, while they must be quite visible to running fish much of the time, any number of bears waiting on station is not going to halt the advance. No priority, in nature, is higher than the urge to breed, and few creatures demonstrate this more vividly than Atlantic salmon.

The Glencar Hotel today has German ownership, bringing clientele from that country to visit Ireland, not just for the fishing. While I was there in August, a party of about twenty ladies from Munich were installed, active during the day hiking in the mountains, a couple turning up to watch me fish the river. Sadly I failed to show them how it should be done, but did explain, in my schoolboy German, what and why I was doing with such enthusiasm, and how exciting it all could be! What was more, we all agreed that fresh wild salmon 'sind zher gute zum essen' was better than farmed fish.

One cannot make a valuable judgement on the Glencar river system without a serious visit during the spring – and the season starts on 17 January, with often a lot of snow on the tops. Good sized fish, averaging 12/13lb, are the order of the day, and with reasonable weather conditions – meaning not too cold – I gathered mid-March to mid-April are likely to produce the best returns. Fish of over 20lb are common, and I would be busy with a fly on both the big lake and the river, in most conditions. Until you have landed a fresh springer, preferably on a fly, you have no idea of how special is this fish, and the general experience.

Somehow one of these days, I will get back to the Glencar River in the spring, if only to show them that the fly is not dead and buried!

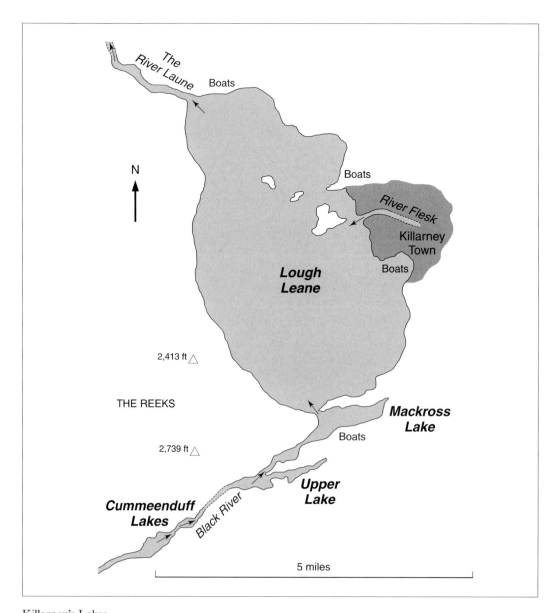

The
River Laune

Boats

N

Boats

River Flesk

Killarney
Town

Boats

Lough
Leane

2,413 ft △

THE REEKS

Mackross
Lake

2,739 ft △

Boats

Upper
Lake

Cummeenduff
Lakes

Black River

5 miles

Killarney's Lakes

Chapter 5

River Laune and the Killarney Lakes

It may not sound a very friendly thing to say, but it looks to me as though this great Irish fishery is only a shadow of what it could be, and that the authorities have little understanding of how much a fully re-vitalised fishery might contribute to tourism. Not that Ted O'Riordan does not understand exactly the possibilities that exist. As secretary of the Laune Salmon and Trout Anglers Association for some years he is as well briefed as anybody. What seems to me to be needed now is something like the Foyle Fisheries Commission, with an independent statutory role to reflect both its catchment of 320 square miles, and more to the point the remarkable assets that are involved. And by that I mean the system has just about everything a salmon fishery needs in great quantity – upper lakes and spawning streams by the score, a very large main lough to provide salmon, sea trout and brown trout fishing, combined with a critical contribution as a vast water reserve against summer drought – and a fine big lower river, a lot of it first class fly water.

In particular the removal of the off-shore nets would benefit here, their immediate area having a 30,000 salmon catch allocation, hitting a summer fishery like this particularly hard. Indeed there is now no spring run worth speaking of, although I am certain there once was so that, particularly by developing the upper lakes – much loved by spring fish – early salmon runs could be restored. Currently almost all spawning takes place in the Flesk river which drains into Lough Leane. In an effort to constrain the 'fishmongering' tendencies of some anglers, Ted told me that his association had tried to have all use of prawns and shrimps banned by law on the Laune which proposal was turned down flat, for no particular reason.

I have never fished the lakes or the river, but have talked to many who have over the years, Noel Huggard being well informed on the River Laune, where he once witnessed a salmon behave in a remarkable manner. He had gone with a friend staying at the Butlers Arms to fish a middle stretch of the river just below a bridge and he started off by casting a fly from the right bank. It was summer and the water was low so that Noel, with his friend's wife up on the bridge watching, could see every pebble on the river bottom easily, its width at that point some eighty yards.

The fisherman had worked his small low water fly out in the normal manner, about twenty yards of line on the water, when the watchers saw from the bridge a salmon leave its lie at the opposite side of the river, swim steadily towards the fly as it drifted with the current, grab it and head for home! It was firmly hooked, landed and weighed in at about 8lb.

All of which would have been a seemingly routine event for the angler himself,

Black River – top of the Laune system

who had not witnessed the remarkable distance the fish had covered to reach the fly. Say its lie was ten yards from the left bank, while with the leader plus a bit of wading the fly had landed thirty yards from the right bank. In that case the fish had spotted the fly some forty yards away, being so attracted by it that it felt a forty yard trip worth while in order to investigate, and no food motive could have been involved. Above all therefore that salmon's eyesight must have been astonishing, even for clear water on a bright day.

Those who have followed these pages so far will know that my love of lough fishing is matched by my feelings relating to the use of fly whenever possible. That this was the method in common use up to the mid-1930s was probably attributable mainly to the then absence of the outboard motor – and that meant on big loughs two oarsmen to propel the long and heavy boats required to cope with large waves. Then first came very basic motors, often hard to start, very different to the excellent products

Lough Leane – 4500 acres

of today, some designed to tick over endlessly at low revs, pushing a troller's boat along without oiling-up, or stalling. The method catches a lot of fish with ease, so that any old passenger who has never fished before can catch a salmon, which widens the market and brings more trade. But it is in fact the boatman who catches the fish, while the passenger only lands it, and the art of fishing is in the catching – landing is simple routine stuff.

Thus, when you have a huge lake like Lough Leane, 4500 acres in size, combined with a similarly large non-fishing tourist trade to satisfy, as happens at Killarney, one can see just why trolling has taken over. That said, given that good brown trout fly fishing is to be had, casting a fly is not entirely a forgotten art.

Much, very rightly, is made of the quite amazing beauty of the Killarney lakes, their castles, and the great swathes of woodlands planted by the aristocracy of old and maintained now thanks to the tourist spending. While the big lake with its steamer

The Reeks – Ireland's highest mountains

Middle Laune – good fly water

trip has wonderful views up to the mountains, if you get in your car and explore up into the Reeks you will do even better. And if you are young and active, on a fine day you can park the car to climb the hills yourself, where you will have a fine view out over the ocean, while looking down on Killarney and its lakes, or west over to Glencar. Never try this in bad weather without a competent local guide, and do not forget your camera.

Meanwhile in terms of angling, the route to the upper lakes starts with Mackross – or the Middle Lake – beside the road to Kenmare, being part of the Ring of Kerry. Next comes the Upper Lake, long and narrow with huge rocks on its shoreline, left smooth and rounded by the ice, for this surely was the path of a glacier. This looks a first class mountain salmon lake, a typical home for spring fish, and once was. Then lastly, as you continue up the Black Valley you arrive at two, also typically glacial lakes, the Cummeenduff Loughs, which are the end of the line for migratory fish.

To get this far means several miles of very minor road leading you into the heart of mountains that need to be taken seriously. Here on the wrong sort of day you wouldn't dream of launching a boat, although these are quite small lakes, which on a fine day with the great hills all round you make a truly inspiring setting. The alternative point of entry is via a famous pass, the Gap of Dunloe, which I think still requires one to leave the car and walk the last mile or so. The approach is from the north-west, with the sea behind one.

Lastly on the Killarney fishing picture, one cannot ignore the River Flesk which, since it provides the bulk of the spawning facilities needed for the system most certainly has plenty of salmon running its waters. Strangely its potential as a fishery is very largely ignored, although there are nearly thirty miles of river involved. Various association waters exist, and some hotel water I was told could be worth a try, while this also had once had a spring run. Again, with a properly managed fishery restoration programme one wonders just what might be made of the Flesk fishery.

The Upper Lake, Killarney

Cummeenduff Lough – the highest salmon lough

How many salmon are taken from the whole system, as often is the case, seems to be largely a well kept secret. Ted's association, which includes nine clubs, average 320 a season on their leased waters, while what happens elsewhere is a guess. However everyone seems to believe that trolling the lakes produces a lot of fish, plus some large ferox trout from time to time.

I end where I began by saying that in my view the River Laune could match any river in Ireland as a salmon fly fishery, while the upper lakes must also have great scope. But a major, well co-ordinated development plan, to run for twenty years, is essential.

Kylemore Abbey

Chapter 6

Connemara

Let us assume we have been in Kerry for a couple of weeks and it is time to move north as the wild geese and eider ducks do in the spring. We will follow the coast to Connemara, taking our time which is always worth while in Ireland, soaking up the beauty of the green, the mountains and the sea – why hurtle through it to leave such a picture a blur?

Then, from the angler's viewpoint, the old military adage that 'time spent on reconnaissance is seldom wasted' is also a factor. There are major rivers you must cross, and freak geological regions where fat trout grow, or remote 'fishy-looking' lakes at the side of the road, with a couple of well kept boats on the shore to make one wonder about whose fishing it is, and everywhere in Ireland there seems to be water. While the impatient traveller, bent on getting to his destination as quickly as possible, may claim such philandering is just a waste of time, all I can say is that the best fishermen I ever met always had a great feeling for country, and environment, and how all creatures fitted in with it.

From Killarney to Galway, the gateway to Connemara, is about three hours on the main roads in normal conditions, and indeed it is a great scythe through the south-west that you would make – being a lot more hilly than one might have guessed, as you travel initially to Limerick. But why not take a bit longer, and go first to Tralee and head north a few miles to the ferry over the Shannon estuary at Tarbert, crossing to Killimer? Here you will disembark into what is a geological freak, the Burren – a sea level alpine garden of limestone – and genuinely unique. There, if you make your visit in springtime, you will be amazed at the variety of unexpected wild flowers growing at the roadside – not unlike a visit to the Scilly Isles off Cornwall – but here mountain plants left behind when the ice withdrew, having covered Ireland one hundred per cent from north to south.

As we travel from central Kerry to Connaught the geology changes mightily beneath us from largely old red sandstone to more than one carboniferous rock type. Then as we near Galway we meet the great plate of pure limestone that covers most of central Ireland, while along the north shore of Galway Bay appear solid igneous and volcanic rocks, as old as any on earth, and completely different.

There is no need to have a degree in geology to appreciate all of this, but it is a help to have a look in a decent atlas to see – literally – how the land lies. And from all of this, you the fisherman will deduce with ease that, for the fish you expect to lure to your fly, the water environment will reflect very precisely the type of host rock present. For rich lime-dominated waters mean plenty of invertebrates, and therefore

The Dawross drains the Kylemore Loughs

ample food supplies, while the sour granites with their peat bogs in Connemara offer the reverse, driving juvenile fish to sea to find food.

In our case our fist stop is to be Ballynahinch Castle with its famous fishery, three quarters of the way from Galway to the western tip of the Connemara peninsula. But again as we have plenty of time, we will make a bit of a detour up the east side of the great Lough Corrib, looked at in detail later. This is pure limestone country, a mass of islands in the lake, stone walls round the fields for the hunters to jump for this is also the home of the famous Galway Blazers pack of foxhounds. It is thirty miles to Cong at the far end, and on the way you will pass, from time to time, the remains of stone castles, built by the Normans who a thousand years ago took over this fertile stretch of Ireland as one of their prime targets.

Beyond Cong is Lough Mask, the two connected by an underground river that has eaten its way through the limestone, so that while salmon come up into Corrib in numbers and spawn, Lough Mask is out of reach. Nor is Corrib itself looked upon as a salmon lough for it is a truly great brown trout lake. After passing through the famous Galway fishery right in the town, the fish spread out to run a variety of feeder rivers, to east, north and west.

We on our tour will go west from Cong into Joyces country, heading for an eight mile finger of sea, Killary Harbour, that curiously appears like some huge canal to divide the county of Galway from Mayo, a waterway which on its tides from January to October will carry many hundreds of salmon and sea trout to the Erriff River, and the Delphi system with its chain of famous loughs which we will visit. This is spectacular country, and as you come down to Leenane the Mweelrea Mountains are facing you, rising up to 2618ft (819m) but looking far higher because they are so close to the sea!

Turning left on the Clifden road, you pass the Kylemore loughs and their greystone convent, shortly to be faced with the true ocean, a shoreline eaten away by the constant rollers, little bays and estuaries. And always to your left are 'The Twelve Pins' a massive granite block that runs up to 2395ft (730m), the oldest rocks of them all, and the central magnet for incoming clouds to drench their tops with rain to fill the rivers.

After Clifden and heading east on the coast road, at a bridge, suddenly you are by a river on your left with someone fishing, and up in the trees the castle of Ballynahinch. You have arrived in time to unpack, prior to a drink and dinner, plus a chat with gillies and anglers in the bar, to get up to date on what is going on. While a lot of the system includes famous loughs, at Ballynahinch at the bottom end next to the sea it is primarily salmon in the river you will be after, although plenty of sea trout are there too. Here a fisherman wakes early on his first morning!

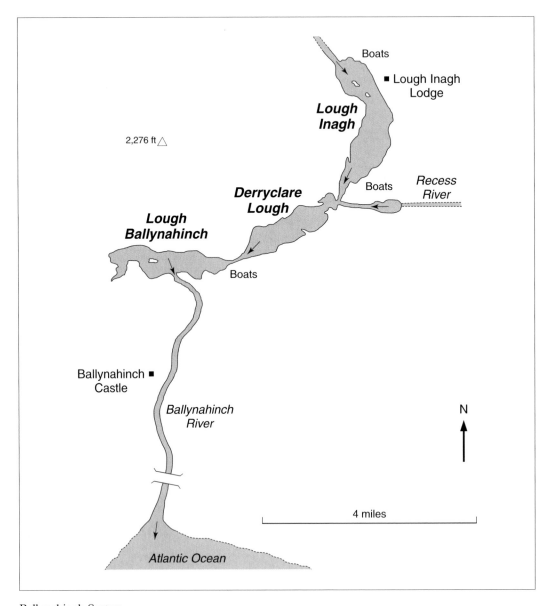

Ballynahinch System

Chapter 7

The Ballynahinch System

Taken against the size typical with most salmon rivers, which are great powerful waters for great strong fish, those found in Connemara are remarkably small, with even the largest, at Ballynahinch, a mere stream against its typical Scottish equivalents. Most of the other rivers of Connemara – even smaller – are primarily sea trout fisheries, while Ballynahinch alone, at one time, proved itself to be a first rate salmon fishery producing prior to the huge increase in the offshore net catches of three hundred to four hundred salmon and grilse in most years. That the total since 1990 has averaged only about seventy-five fish is a shocking reflection on how lack of government control – nets take eighty per cent of returning salmon – can do such serious damage. At the same time the salmon farming industry was allowed to set up in business on their doorstep, which, while terminal for sea trout, also damages the salmon's chances, thanks to the associated sea lice plague. It was therefore fantastic news to be told on arriving at the castle that the year 2001 had seen a massive improvement in sea trout numbers, including some truly remarkable catches, with one rod landing thirty in an evening, and another twenty-six, while ten or a dozen was par for the course.

The history of Ballynahinch is highly romantic and a long way from run of the mill, it being owned by a variety of distinguished families and individuals starting with the O'Flaherty clan. Go back to Grace O'Malley who had married into the O'Flahertys – 'the pirate queen of Connaught' – in 1593 she met Queen Elizabeth I of England, head to head as monarch to monarch, speaking Latin, it being their easiest common language, prompting the contemporary comment, 'in the wild grandeur of her mien erect and high before the English Queen she dauntless stood!'

At this time the O'Flaherty family were still owners of the property, but it changed hands in 1586 when the Bingham family took over by force. Sir Richard Bingham, the governor of Connaught – Grace O'Malley's greatest enemy – placed his brother, Captain John Bingham, as his area lieutenant in charge of Ballynahinch, seizing the livestock, 'four thousand cattle, five hundred stud mares and horses, and a thousand sheep' – to quote the castle's official history. This was a centre of economic activity, and an important place.

The Martin family arrived in the area in 1590 at Ross outside Galway, subsequently acquiring the Ballynahinch estate. Some of the present house was built about 1700 as an inn, and in 1754 Richard Martin was born. Richard Martin was a friend of the Prince Regent and as a Member of Parliament was the first person to introduce legal rights for animals with his 1822 'Cruelty to Animals Act', earning

Ballynahinch Castle

him the name 'Humanity Dick'. This lead to the formation of the Society for the Prevention of Cruelty to Animals – still in existence today as the RSPCA.

Dick Martin was, however, very far from being a soft hearted, or gentle, individual, known in his earlier years as 'Hair-Trigger Dick', having a great appetite for duelling. He gave lavish parties, and frequently fell out with his father, at one point locking him up in a prison, located on an island in the middle of a lake! It is said that after his death, during the potato famine, the family more or less made themselves bankrupt by selling everything they owned to help feed the starving thousands in their area and the estate was subsequently sold to the Berridge family.

The estate was vast, including both Upper and Lower Ballynahinch lakes, plus Loughs Derryclare and Inagh. The next owner was the famous Indian maharajah Ranjitsinhji, known by all as 'Ranji', one of the world's greatest cricketers. He was hugely rich, with estates in England as well, and at the end of each season in Ireland gave the local population the five motorcars he had bought in Galway on arrival! Ranji, bought the estate in 1924 and spent a fortune on creating a huge garden, while transforming much of the river by introducing numerous piers and casting platforms. Sadly he died in 1932 and his nephew Dulipsinhji owned it for only a short time before selling to the McCormacks from Dublin. The Tourist Board took over in 1946, attracting a host of celebrities, while keeping the place alive and in good order which was no mean task in post-war Europe.

In the 1950s Noel Huggard, whom we met at Waterville, took charge of the management and in line with a government policy that favoured reduction in size of the great estates (many owned by Anglo-Irish families who lived in the United Kingdom) Huggard sold a very considerable proportion of the land involved, together with Lough Inagh and the Derryclare lake, being persuaded himself to sell the castle and the remaining property – as he put it to me – at a price that nobody in their right mind could have refused. Edward Ball was the buyer, an American businessman, who formed a company to own and manage the operation, subsequently selling shares in it to a number of friends, and attracting President Gerald Ford, and British Prime Minister Jim Callaghan to stay as guests.

Lough Inagh – top of the system

The Ballynahinch River

As a country hotel it is as good as one can get, having immaculate formal public rooms with an amazing view from the dining room that looks over the river, where with your breakfast you can see salmon and sea trout rising and splashing about. Meanwhile the large bar, where less formal meals are provided, is relaxed and full of fishermen and gillies in the evening, offering local advice and help for strangers.

On my recent trip I was there from 1 to 3 September in not very good fishing conditions, the violent wind making accurate casting far from easy. I fished two adjacent beats, not far above the tide, immediately below the old railway bridge, catching and returning some small sea trout, with a couple of pulls that might have been salmon, using at that point a sinking line with a large prawn fly attached. I was on my own at the time, and had no idea that the place this occurred was a well established lie, being in one of the very slow moving canal-like stretches which can fish remarkably well in a wind, the bob fly playing a major part. I saw a number of quite large salmon jump, one absolutely fresh at about 12lb, a good sized summer fish which are quite common, and a welcome change from the swarms of tiny grilse that seem to have taken over in western Ireland. Given the offshore regulations mean nets with fairly large dimension modules, from which small grilse can escape, one wonders if we are not suffering as a result.

Thanks to the massive input from Ranji this river is very largely easy to fish, and ideal for the more elderly angler – such as myself. With excellent access to most of the pools, to get a fly in exactly the right place is seldom a problem, albeit, since long casting may be required from time to time, the wind can prove a serious difficulty, there being minimal cover in a lot of places. The upper river, and the other estates, have good spawning facilities, thanks to the loughs' good reserves of water, which drain an area of 68 square miles of outstanding, rugged, beauty.

The fishery is fly only in almost all circumstances, a very substantial rise in the water needed to allow the use of a spinner, although because of the loughs above, even in flood the water is almost never badly coloured, and a large tube fly can be employed where appropriate.

Action on Beat 6

So much for the Ballynahinch river – more correctly yet another Owenmore – but there are no less than eight different fisheries within the system, including three loughs of considerable size, supported by a number of smaller lakes. Working from the bottom of the river upwards the first major lough is the Ballynahinch Lake, owned by the castle and also referred to as the Lower Lake, followed by Derryclare Lough, while at the top is Lough Inagh. These were all superb sea trout lakes prior to the crisis, with good numbers of heavier fish to lift the average weight. They also produced large numbers of salmon to the fly, for this is not trolling water, having also some remarkable fishing from the shore at the butts which is the point of entry of the feeder rivers.

The concept of fishing those places in lakes where fish congregate is clearly sensible, and as we saw at Currane the bay where the Cummeragh River enters is a prime location for anglers, being very obviously an area where fish waiting to run a spawning stream will be found. On small rivers that contain numerous lakes, these provide the best waiting environment, and it follows that such river mouths will play an important role, with the point of entry quite fishable from the land. So, rather as you might on a large river, one fishes from the shore, as a sort of bastard operation. When starting up stream you are in a river, but as you work your way towards the open lake down the river it widens, and the flow rate slows, until almost no current is discernible as the lough takes over.

As we saw with Lough Namona at Waterville, and will discover elsewhere, these waters are prolific producers of fish and popular with salmon in particular. What is more they will lie extremely close to the shore so that your approach to start with must involve great caution. Do not think however that you will only get fish close to a stream's point of entry, as where a rocky shore stretches away from the entry point, often for two hundred yards or so, you will find salmon lying. I have always found they like weed beds presumably to give them a source of cover from above if needed. With sea trout the position is different as they are not likely to lie really close in, although within ten yards of a rocky lee shore seems to attract larger fish in a good wave, as we discovered on Derriana.

Butts therefore are interesting places with, particularly in a wind, a two-handed rod a real advantage, for once out on the shore of the lake you will want to fish far off, as well along the rocks close in. In fact as I mentioned, the sea trout tend to be much further from the shore than salmon, so that this is not the place for a typical, light line, boat rod. I also believe that a sinking line can be an asset, particularly at night when the butts at Derryclare can produce remarkable sport.

Of the major lakes, I have only fished Lough Inagh, the top lake on the main river, and that was on a couple of visits a good many years ago, when there were plenty of sea trout to be found. On both occasions we had good baskets of fish, although being in August their size was small. Inagh has its own variation of the Bibio, designed I believe to be more eye-catching than the standard pattern, its central segment being a bright, quite pale red, while the normal thin wire round the body is

Approaching Lough Inagh

replaced by bands of silver tinsel. Exactly as I prefer Black Pennels which have the same characteristics, being excellent on major waters like Currane, I think the Lough Inagh Bibio is a great fly for a big wave, and on a dark day.

Early in the season the butts are of particular interest to the salmon angler, as the big springers, up to 20lb being quite common, head rapidly up to these upper fisheries with, in good conditions in March a real chance, and plenty about in April and May. June is the month for the big trout and the start of the grilse run, while the smaller sea trout come into the system on every high tide. With their numbers in the year 2001 on the increase – and this year's 'juniors' become next year's adult fish – it may be that this once unique fishery will be back to its old remarkable capacity before long!

Turning east towards Maam Cross, following the Clifden to Galway main road, you will see beside you a chain of loughs, drained by a series of small rivers all part of the Ballynahinch system. These tributaries enjoy an excellent run of sea trout, with a few salmon, access in most cases easy to negotiate. The top lake is Lough Oorid, being as one would expect at its best in August and September. I fished it once in July catching a number of brown trout, somewhat to my surprise, for I was too early for migratory fish.

Too much sun

A good wind for fishing

The scope and size of the Ballynahinch system is remarkable, with a chance that it will now make a spectacular comeback as its sea trout return. To go with it there are hotels, houses and cottages to rent, with no shortage of 'B&B' facilities. I have not stayed there but recently called in at the Lough Inagh Lodge Hotel for a chat while passing, and for anglers on that lake it seemed to me perfect – a few minutes from its shore. Their fishery is more comprehensive than many, comprising Loughs Inagh and Derryclare, with their connecting Inagh River, and of course those butts. The hotel was a fishing lodge for the Berridge family and has a lot to offer the angler.

The ancient rocks of Connemara are the base for its major fishery and system – the mountains bring the rain for the rivers – the rivers bring the fish – and it looks as though it is improving!

The little Gowla River

Chapter 8

Gowla and Others

Travel east from Ballynahinch along the coast road, with Galway Bay to your right, and a fisherman's progress will resemble the stop-start of an underground, or subway train, for every few miles there is a bridge over a small river which anglers must get out to inspect. There are no less than six little but fishable systems involved to be crossed in the following order – Gowla, Invermore, Inverbegh, Screeb, Fermoyle Costello and lastly Spiddal. In addition there are a few even smaller streams, where in high water some white trout – and even a stray salmon – can nip up from the sea to a little lough, until it is time to spawn.

Of the six systems I have personal experience of only two, the Gowla with one visit and the Costello and Fermoyle fishery with five. I am therefore dealing with the latter in a single chapter, and the other five collectively.

Against even the modest sized Ballynahinch system these little rivers are tiny, so that your average salmon fisherman used to Scottish, let alone Norwegian rivers, will find it hard to think of such streams as capable of holding the king of fish, although fitting for sea trout. However, while fish numbers are not on the scale of the Galway River which indeed is of Scottish proportions – catchment 1212 square miles with a big run of salmon starting in February – I have seen at Costello surprising numbers of fish in July and August.

But perhaps the most remarkable feature of these southern slopes of central Connemara is the astonishing number of loughs, appearing on the map in places as half land and half water. On the ground tiny trickles drain the peat bogs, amalgamating to feed a series of just descending loughs that get bigger progressively, linked by streams to become rivers that feed the tide. However up these systems, that in low water are little more than seepage, the white trout will fight their way after rain, right to the very top, to Lough Shanawona at the source of the Costello River, or the School House Loughs on the same system but east, the entry stream looking in August both too steep and too small for access ever to be possible. But, the white trout get there in modest numbers as you will discover when you offer them a fly in reasonable conditions, and your expedition can be an interesting alternative to yet another day on the lough, however good or much fun that is.

Throughout the area an even more remarkable feature is the massive carpet of rocks, a moonscape of granite boulders, many as big as a house, left by the retreating ice as the cap withdrew north. And yet again what a great geology lesson it all is, the acidic southern slopes, home to the little river systems, producing minimal food for the juvenile white trout and salmon after hatching, home to stunted brownies that go six to the pound. Then take the road from Costello to Oughterard, up over the featureless mass of granite that makes Iar Connaught an independent region in itself, and see the country change when you are over the top, to descend to the plains of Lough Corrib, we looked at on our way from Kerry. See the lush green grass, the neat limestone walled fields, and note the chain of intervisible stone towers, built by the Normans who knew a bit about where to concentrate their farming efforts, as well as how to fight off the locals, upset by the loss of their best grazing. With their towers placed so they could communicate visually, if one keep was attacked it could signal its neighbours to form an amalgamated, and much larger force to deal with the attackers.

But let's get back to the white trout systems, and those six bridges we were stopping at, these are ninety-five per cent sea trout and only five per cent salmon fisheries. While the Ballynahinch lakes, right up to Lough Inagh, have plenty of salmon, these others earned their fame not as salmon fisheries, but as top class white trout fisheries, with salmon taken, largely after a good spate. This makes these little systems nearly unique, in much the same way that the Hebridean islands have fisheries that are in a class of their own. In both cases loughs/lochs play a major role for salmon and sea trout fishermen, having as common factors their extreme westward location, the paucity of their peat stained waters, and how best to catch fish!

The first river one meets on our eastward journey is the Gowla, draining a series of sixteen loughs into Betraghboy Bay. In 1974 I stayed at the Zetland Hotel, at Cashel, which owns the fishery, from 8 to 17 August, and in my nine days, with a great deal of heavy rain and gales, netted fifty-six sea trout, best 4¼lb, but on average only about ¾lb. A month earlier, I was assured, and I would have had fewer but larger fish.

By far the most important lake is Gowla Lough – more correctly Loughanillann – about three miles up from the sea, which gets going in late June with big white trout, and salmon on a flood from then on. It is hugely fragmented into bays and arms, with an almost cut-off eastern section. There are plenty of islands, and there was hardly anywhere that did not produce a trout or two, and fished with light tackle it was great fun.

The upper lakes clearly need water to get fish up, but are well worth a visit, particularly by younger anglers more able to cover the bogs to get there with alacrity. Many were very lightly fished when I was there, while the river itself from Gowla Lough down to the sea, has considerable scope, where I hooked and lost a salmon. The river has plenty of pools which in this environment means those curious long almost canal-like stretches which fish well in a good wind. In fact the best technique is, with an upriver wind, to cast with the wind and across, and retrieve one's flies exactly as one would from a boat on a lough – the bobfly cutting the surface and all!

Gowla Lake – typical of Connemara's best

I had a very ancient gillie who shortly before I arrived had caught the largest sea trout taken for many years from the Gowla, from the main lake, at just under 6lb. In the gales the boat, no outboards allowed then, was too much for him and half a day was enough. A French angler from Brittany – interested to hear I came from Cornwall – who owned a tackle shop in Rennes was intrigued by the numbers of trout I netted, never himself having fished from a boat before. I tried in schoolboy French to explain the techniques involved, being rather pleased with my 'Daddy Long Legs' translation! You work it out.

I loved my ten days at the hotel, where the side bar was full of people, and music, and late nights, and I called in the other day. It has moved up market but remains an excellent fisherman's base.

As I have never fished the next three fisheries my opinions are far less personal.

However the first, Invermore, has a very considerable reputation for producing above average weight trout, plus salmon in good conditions. Quite near the road, Invermore Lough is at the bottom of the system, followed by other well known names including Lough Aliggan (or Luggeen), Curreal, Owengarve (Shanaket), Cuskematinny (Cushmeg) and Loughannemlagh (Emlough East) working inland to the headwaters. One day in late July, I will somehow have a go on these loughs, and I bet the action will be fast and furious, including given some rain, salmon to go with above average size trout.

Then comes the Inverbegh system which is a rather smaller and private fishery. I once had a drink and chat with the owners, and was left in no doubt that if you can get a day or two on the fishery you should grab the chance with both hands, the benefit from being relatively under-fished a major advantage. As with its neighbours, it is a mix of river with pools, and lough fishing, the latter having butts at the point of river entry, usually being hot salmon lies. One oddity that sticks in my mind was being told that as an experiment they had tried tying the bob fly at the point where line meets nylon. It worked well!

The Screeb fishery, is the next system, and, for no obvious reason a larger producer of salmon as against white trout than any of the other five small systems. To a degree this visibly reflects an environment which is more 'salmony', with the famous Screeb Butt where the river enters Screeb Lake, a massive three hundred yards of most fishable water. Described as 'one of the best pools in the west of Ireland' by Peter O'Reilly, he reports that during his 1988 visit fifty-eight fish were taken in seventy-three rod days!

For years a private fishery, Screeb is now a traditional fishing hotel, not unlike the Zetland, and for those interested in taking salmon from small loughs, one of the best bets going.

Here we will bypass Costello for the moment, dealt with in the next chapter in some detail, including a visit on my recent trip. One should however make the point that for those not wedded entirely to fishing – as some of us are – a day out on the Aran Islands, going either by air or boat, is something well worth doing.

Which leaves the last leg of the drive to Galway and these days the coast road is becoming increasingly built upon as the prosperity of Ireland shows its hand. About ten miles short of the city is the village of Spiddal, historic home of the Morris family whose most famous member in recent years was Lord Killanin, guide and mentor of the Olympic movement. The little River Spiddal has a run of trout and salmon draining two main loughs, Boliska and Derryherk, and a number of smaller lakes up the system. The country is slightly less wild than the moonscape of Cashla and considerable efforts to improve the fishing are currently in hand. This once was a famous fishery, and looks as though it may be about to make a serious comeback.

Although next we will return to Costello, so ends my trip along the north shore of

Galway Bay, with its bridges over the little white trout and salmon rivers. In fishing terms, don't compare it with the Tweed or the Towy, it is utterly different – think of Skye and Harris – while just as different is the art form required to catch the silver fish that come in with the tide. One day, maybe quite soon the sea trout crisis will be resolved, and when it is the glories of these perfect miniature fisheries will again emerge in their true lights. May it be soon.

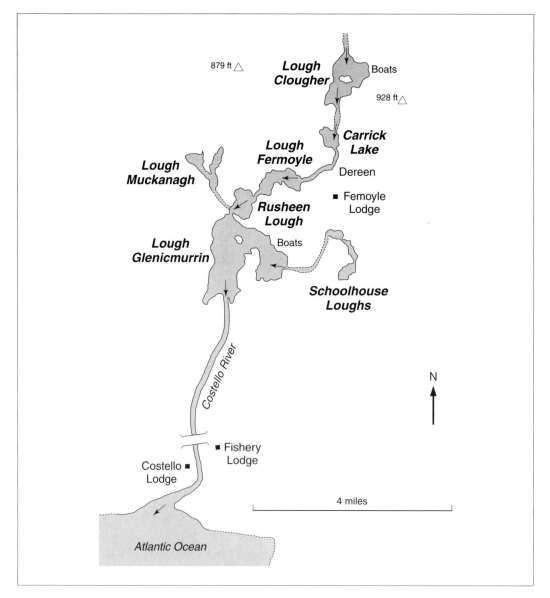

Costello and Fermoyle

Chapter 9

Costello and Fermoyle

To return to the Cashla River, this embraces two famous fisheries long since amalgamated, Costello at the lower end, and Fermoyle above, the particular white trout 'Shangri La' for the High Court judge T.C. Kingsmill Moore who recorded his experiences in great detail in his superb book *A Man May Fish*. It is a superb fishery that I have visited several times, the first immediately after my 1974 efforts on the Gowla. By the same token, including a wide range of weather conditions, between 17 and 25 August I kept sixty-two white trout, the best 3lb, with average weight just below 1lb per trout, returning a lot more very small ones.

I had one exceptional day fishing with Pat Walsh as my boatman on Beat 3 of Lough Glenicmurrin (Costello Lake). Pat fished some of the time, getting eight trout of the twenty-five we kept with another four very small trout returned. My notes, made at the time say, 'bright, firm wind south a.m. – strong south west p.m. – best 2¾lb – 3 × 2lb – Black Pennel, Bibio, Gold Butcher'. Curiously, despite the high numbers we felt throughout the day that we should have been doing better, possibly because the average weight was low, just below 1lb, with no salmon seen, again typical August. However with very light tackle it certainly was great sport and a day very well remembered.

As a curious contrast the two following days were entirely different, first on little Lough Rusheen the lough next up river, where in heavy rain and rising water, I rose seventeen trout plus a salmon at the butt and netted exactly two! Then even worse next day, back on Beat 1 of Glenicmurrin, my notes say this 'Came short all day – rose 32 – netted 4 – hooked and lost a further 6 – day looked good but cold – wind backed to south-east!'

During my visit I rose six salmon in total, hooked and lost three, but failed to net one, mostly due to quick striking, which the sea trout require. Since those days I have done a lot more salmon fishing in loughs and am sure that today my results would be much improved!

Looking at the fishery from bottom to top, there is about two miles of excellent river fishing leading from the sea pool at Costello Lodge, close to the road bridge, working in comfortable steps up to Glenicmurrin, the largest lough in the system, and first stop for every single fish returning from the sea. A very few spring salmon come each year, with the total salmon average about sixty fish, but the end of June sees a big influx of grilse alongside the larger white trout. However in terms of numbers it is from the end of July onwards that huge numbers of small trout, the 'harvesters' or 'juniors' weighing only ½ to ¾lb pour in on every tide.

The Cabbage Pool – Costello River

Where the river leaves the lough an early experiment with the use of artificial spates took place, as Kingsmill Moore, in *A Man May Fish* reports. 'As far back as 1833, when an English fisherman visited our waters . . . (he) was told one rod had killed over two hundred trout in a day. He himself caught thirty-five trout running up to five pounds on his first day, and twenty-seven trout and two salmon the next'. He says that there were gratings at the head of the river, and sluices at the mouth of the lake, making it a completely artificial environment in which great slaughter occurred.

Above this in two basic sections, including a great many side bays, rocks and islands, Lough Glenicmurrin itself has four boats, but I have never seen more than three being fished at one time. On the central island is an excellent and solid stone hut with a fireplace, providing welcome shelter from an Atlantic storm. In fishing terms the lough is at its best in July before all the larger trout have moved on to the upper loughs, which given rain they will do quickly. Adjacent to the main lake are Cloonadoon and Muckanagh, neither of which has the quality of fishing found in the main series of loughs, such as Rusheen, quite small and next up the system. Then comes famous Lough Fermoyle, considerably larger and with a variety of fishing characteristics, including some notably shallow areas, good salmon points on the south side, and an excellent butt for salmon, which is immediately below a sizeable fall, the system's largest. In fact it takes a considerable weight of water to get fish up over this obstacle, and not just an ordinary small spate. Thanks to this the number of fish in the lough below can build up to considerable proportions, with in good conditions excellent fishing, particularly in mid-July when the larger trout and salmon are fresh arrivals.

Next and no distance upstream is a truly curious little lough, Dereen, only a few acres in size and arguably, after a good flood has enabled the fish to get up from Fermoyle, one of the most prolific stillwater fisheries anywhere, producing both trout and salmon.

Fish counter – Costello

The Cottage Pool – Costello

After this is Carrickillawallia, surrounded by boulder-strewn hillsides, feeling rather like a staging post as the river climbs up into the hills. It is about half the size of Fermoyle, deep in places and has a good salmon lie where the river enters. To continue on up river you will find on the two mile stretch leading to Lough Ailogher (Clougher) several good pools – similar to those in the Gowla – canal like, deep and slow flowing. The judge, with reference to the Clougher Pool illustration in his book, says that 'it shows all the characteristic dullness and featurelessness of a first-class white trout pool'. With wind they fish remarkably well, but on a calm bright day are a waste of time until late into the evening. After a flood such pools can fish well for salmon, particularly right in the neck.

As the last major lough Clougher itself nearly 500ft (152m) up produced for Kingsmill Moore some remarkable days being for him the system's greatest challenge. The trout so high up are much larger on average, it is a good salmon lough, but you certainly need a boatman to guide you. It has two clearly different halves, an island with a hut on it, and it is remote – small mountains to both the north-west and south-east. You are a long way from the soft life of Glenicmurrin, and perhaps it is the altitude, for the fish can be rising well at one moment and completely dead the next. But it is a great wild and truly inspiring place to be fishing for the wildest of fish.

Although there is the Lough Shanawona a mile on above Clougher, the latter is the last serious lough on the system, which is for me, as it was for the judge, the complete small fishery, one you can know from top to bottom, having a great variety of fishing, river and lough, designed to suit all ages. Meanwhile with merlins and ravens and even a few grouse to share the hills with, and the ocean beside you, it's not just fishing.

Fishing the tail of the Cottage Pool

My recent visit was inspiring for a number of reasons but the most important without doubt was the continuous improvement in the sea trout numbers recorded through their fish counter. This is located about half a mile above the tide on the river and has been in place for some years. The current trend shows an annual sea trout increase of at least 1000 a year, 2000 recording 8000 fish in total, while at the beginning of September 2001 some 7000 had passed through, making a total of 10,000 for the year quite possible. Terry Gallaher is now manager coming from the government's Galway team and he says he hopes to see sixty salmon and with luck 2000 sea trout netted for the year by anglers, and this is a strictly fly only fishery. He also gave me the catch returns 1985 to 2000:

Year	Sea Trout	Salmon
1985	2475	21
1986	2316	34
1987	1698	42
1988	1900	74
1989	462	60
1990	406	24
1991	234	12
1992	464	101
1993	699	84
1994	1069	88
1995	634	62
1996	1281	92
1997	676	66
1998	2398	57
1999	1381	53
2000	1604	65

While salmon are relatively constant, the big 1991 drop I suspect was due to far fewer fishermen present. Salmon are a good alternative, not least because you can take them home to eat – for the sea trout all have to be returned. One point from the above to catch the eye is that while some 8000 trout were counted through in the year 2000 the catch was almost exactly twenty per cent, which given the area of the fishery and the number of lakes sounds to me a high level of take – but undoubtedly true!

Back in the 1970s when I was there on several occasions, the fishery was owned by a syndicate and included Costello House, plus its cottage. Today the house has gone and a new company owns and runs it, while Fermoyle Lodge, one of the previous

Terry Gallagher – Lough Glenicmurrin

owners before the amalgamation in the 1960s, is now a private hotel offering 'Country House Accommodation', owned by an enthusiastic French gentleman – a keen angler. It is not part of the fishing company but is perfectly located for the angler who wants rather more than 'B&B'. The house was another of the Berridge family's sporting lodges, thus part of the Ballynahinch estate, and built in 1875.

The prime mover, and managing director of the company that owns the fishery, is Geoffrey Fitzjohn, at Dereen Lodge, whose family owned and lived at Fermoyle Lodge for many years, selling it quite recently. He is a qualified estate agent and manager, having spent most of his working life in Scotland, clearly extremely well informed on lough and river management, and a first class fisherman as well. His mother has built a delightful house, Dereen Lodge, looking down on that very special little lough, where they kindly asked me for supper after Geoffrey and I had fished Clougher.

The lunch hut on the island.

When I was there Clougher had been made even more remote because of work on the forest road that usually gets one quite close. We therefore had a good half hour slog to get there, where we found the lake full of small sea trout, from ½lb to 1½lb, of which we hooked and returned over a dozen in the few hours we fished – about 3 to 6 pm. Nothing could show one more vividly how the numbers of trout were recovering, and here again this year's small fish should return as much larger fish next year. That said Geoffrey told me that earlier in the season a number of good sized sea trout had come off Clougher, which is the normal pattern, as they run in June and I was there in early September.

A lot of work has gone into improving spawning beds, and I gather the worries of damage through encroaching forests have been resolved. Prospects therefore seem most encouraging, and what a boon it would be to get back to the 'status quo' – or better if the drift nets go!

Geoffrey Fitzjohn – a Clougher sea trout

Galway's famous weir

Chapter 10

The Galway Fishery

When a river system drains some 1212 square miles of country which enjoys a high average level of rainfall, the volume of water carried is huge. When this is condensed, shortly before it meets the tide, to flow through a number of gates in the Salmon Weir, the speed of the flow combined with its volume makes this a spectacular place to fish, and with a big spring salmon attached to the end of your line, a formidable environment indeed. For this mass of heavy water is exactly what salmon love, their great strength and special abilities showing to perfection.

It is always interesting, when at a long established fishery such as Galway, to look back at the records of fish taken over the years which so often today, sadly, makes one's mouth water. For instance for the two decades 1881 to 1899 the average catch was 943 salmon, albeit there were huge swings, the take 1720 fish in 1890 against only 221in 1893! This compares with a total for 1999 of 461 salmon and exactly 500 in 2000, of which spring fish were only fifty-six, down from seventy-two the previous year, while June alone saw 317 taken – average 5.45lb – against 293 the year before. Going back a few years the five-year average catch from 1985 to 1989 was 816 salmon, again showing remarkable fluctuations for in 1989 1905 salmon were landed, but only 430 in 1985.

One particular change between now and then is of course the general trend seen everywhere, with numbers of spring salmon – indeed two sea-winter-fish as a whole – falling. Against this one-sea-winter grilse numbers have risen, the combined weight of fish landed being thereby much reduced, a position which appears to be part of a long term pattern, as records on the Tweed, and other well managed fisheries, show in considerable detail.

The popular methods employed here from the weir down are spinner, prawn and fly, while up river in the deep slow waters that lead up to Lough Corrib, trolling with boats takes over. In total from the lake to the tide there are some six miles of river, permits needed only for the stretch from the weir down, the whole managed now by the Western Regional Fisheries Board on behalf of the owners, the Government.

As a matter of purely personal taste this type of fishing is not for me a great attraction. There are, nearly always it seems, far too many people all over the place, and although numbers fishing are limited, while anglers are meant to move down with each cast it is still shoulder to shoulder, albeit in some cases fly takes precedence over other methods. One is also more or less in a built up area – particularly the beats below the Salmon Weir Bridge – with heavy traffic to go with it. That said it is rightly a famous and ancient fishery, so that for those to whom catching salmon is the dominating requirement, the Galway fishery ranks high on the list.

This is not a sea trout fishery of any note, although the lowest town beat accounts for numbers of small fish in the summer with remarkably few found up stream. That however is the classic format where lakes full of rich feeding are available, something that leads to the question – 'are sea trout brown trout that went to sea, or are brown trout sea trout that swam up a river, liked what they found, and stayed?' Bearing in mind that they are in fact an identical species it is a good question, and something similar can be asked of salmon which to me, as with sea trout, certainly do not feel like a salt water, oceanic, species. One thing is certain and that is that when the ice covered the whole of Ireland, together with a mass of European rivers, for a long time many rivers and lakes were wiped out as a suitable home for either species, so that with the thaw their presence needed to be re-introduced. The question therefore arises as to whether the trout could have swum, along side their salmon cousins, from say Spain and Portugal, and southern French rivers, back to habitat once their home for a very long time. Nor should one ignore the fact that the withdrawal of the ice was so recent – only eleven thousand years ago and just yesterday in terms of evolution. I used to believe firmly that sea trout came first from the sea and stayed to take advantage of the environment, but I'm now far less convinced! While presumably all fish at some point came from the sea!

I have looked at the Galway fishery several times over the years, and have always been impressed by its scope as a fly fishery, mainly from the east, left, bank, facing the fisheries board offices, on down to the bridge. While at the top and, immediately below the weir, one's activities are governed by the number of gates open – and with truly high water much of the fly fishing from that side will be restricted – lower down towards the bridge, with wading possible, good coverage of the river is perfectly practicable. Here in the spring I would be fishing a slow sinking line, with nylon of at least 16lb – for a 20lb fresh fish in this water can break you with ease – the lure attached to its end something like a 2½ inch tube fly that, being so close to the sea, had plenty of silver in it. Having said that, I notice that silver is not a feature of the flies recommended in Peter O'Reilly's *Trout and Salmon Rivers of Ireland* which include Garry Dog, Munro Killer, Green Highlander, Willie Gunn, Tosh, and Black Goldfinch, on which he comments that 'dark flies work best in the evening' and adding that fly size is important, down to 10 or 12 for summer grilse.

This in my opinion is not a beat where a single-handed rod is suitable, not even in low water, for good line control is vital if you are to fish the flies correctly at long range. And that certainly means also, chest waders and an effective wading stick, combined with a fair level of fitness and mobility, particularly early in the season.

The opposite bank is entirely different since you are fishing from the wall several feet above the river, but in places a heavy fly rolled out over the stream can be made to fish attractively over the lies. Here the single spey cast comes into its own, and

Below the weir – fishing a fly

thanks to the elevated position works well, as I was able to demonstrate on my last visit. However, for the majority of the run, a spinner, which for me always should be a devon to start with, cast over the current with a long line down stream would be most likely to score as it worked slowly and well sunk back to the bank. Particularly in the cold early months, using weighted devons, deep and slow movement is vital, exactly as one would fish the Cork Blackwater or the lower Tay in Scotland. For this work a multiplier reel is far superior to a fixed spool model, making the whole operation close to fishing a sunk fly with a long line, without the difficulties of recovering the line before each new cast.

Indeed the fishery brings back memories of exactly those spring rivers which have hung on to a spring run somehow, despite much reduced numbers. Straight from the sea in February a 15lb salmon is a truly remarkable prize, silver with a few sea lice attached, it is a glorious form of food, making also the best smoked salmon, a totally different creature to its twin taken in September, only fit to be returned with

At the weir – low water

care and left to spawn. With luck the long term cycle will change again so that grilse numbers will fall while larger two-sea winter salmon will take over. Just that happened between 1880 and 1920, a fact brilliantly illustrated by the records available both at Careysville on the Cork Blackwater, and for the Tweed where the Commissioners have it in black and white. While these changes are slow to occur the scale of the movement is so dramatic I feel readers might care to see the graph as an appendix (see page 195).

There is one point on the fishery, quite common with weir pools, where one finds oneself fishing a bait, spinner or fly in the wrong direction, ie. up stream facing the weir. This is due to the considerable whirlpool effect generated by the central rush of water, leaving a partial vacuum beside it. In this case the position is obvious at a glance as one stands on the wall just below the sluices on the right bank, and it is equally clear that if one were to cast down stream from that point once a spinner was out of the rush below the sluice, as you retrieved next to the wall you would need to wind faster to keep the bait working with the flow coming towards you. All of which sounds complex but is in fact inevitable and clear to the eye on the spot. In these circumstances, with fish lying in the quiet water out of the rush they will be facing down stream so that to present your spinner, or any form of lure, in the correct manner the angler must fish up stream, casting to the edge of the rush and working it back to his bank from right to left as he sees it. Here you can start some fifty yards below the weir and edge your way up, the reverse of normal and a great way to catch fish. In very cold early months very heavy 3 inch devons are ideal, designed almost to bounce off the nose of a comatose salmon that is made slow to react by the conditions.

So much for the bottom part of this major salmon system, next we will look at Lough Corrib and its tributaries where we find that the concept of a great salmon fishery is curiously exchanged for that of a great brown trout fishery, a position repeated with the River Moy and Lough Conn in County Mayo, as we also shall see.

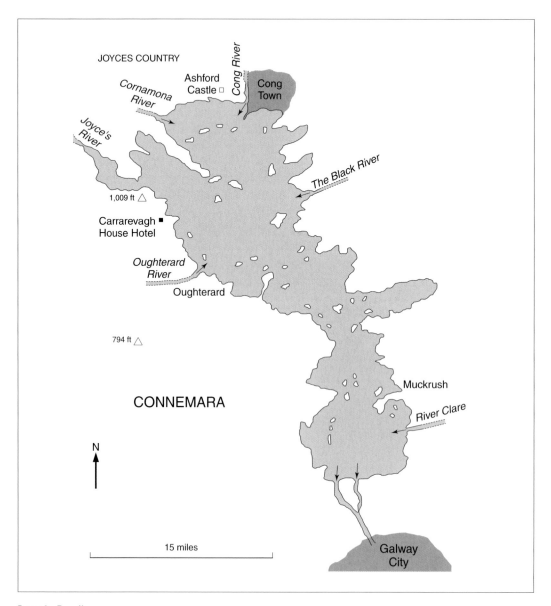

Lough Corrib

Chapter 11

Lough Corrib

When I first planned this book Lough Corrib, or the Corrib as they call it, was not included. To me it is one of the world's great natural brown trout lakes, and although salmon are caught in large numbers, nobody thinks of it as a great salmon fishery, while there are almost no sea trout to be found. It is also so vast, being thirty-five miles in a long arc from end to end, that it feels more like an inland sea, which maybe explains its popular name, rather as the English Channel comes down to the Channel, in both cases an element of affection often implied.

Geographically, when combined with Loughs Mask and Carra to the north, the lakes form a massive block – a moat almost – that divides Connemara from central Ireland, concentrating human movement through Galway city to the south, and Cong to the north. The former was always trade, something that attracted the Normans, but at Cong the old church had a flourishing abbey, active in the sixth century and visited by St Patrick himself. The monks also built, with great ingenuity, in the Cong River a superb fish catching arrangement, made of solid stone and roofed, beneath its floor space room for a slatted trap open at the lower end, the current free to flow through. Exactly how the mechanism worked history does not relate, although it is recorded that by attaching a considerable length of twine to the entry gate, with the arrival of a fish, this caused a bell to ring within the main building – which looked to me at least 150 yards away! Thereby the duty monk, who was keeping warm and out of the rain, grabbed a net, and perhaps a burning torch, to set forth, returning with his catch. Thus the church's requirement that on Fridays only fish, and never meat nor fowl, could pass their lips was supported.

As we saw in Galway this huge drainage area has a tremendous run of salmon, the whole lake being funnelled through that one set of flood gates. The question therefore is where in the inland sea will those salmon be heading in order to spawn? But first a look at the lake in more detail, lying as it does over solid limestone. It has four divisions:

The Lower Lake from Galway up to the point where east and west banks come together at Muckrush.

The Narrows from there up to Oughterard on the west shore and Inchiquin Island to the east.

The Middle Lake being the remainder to the north, with Cong at its centre, but ignoring the long bay, running north west beyond Inishdoorus Island and its next door peninsula.

The Upper Lake, its north-west corner, which stretches right up the latter bay to meet Joyce's River as it flows down from Maam.

Cong Abbey – visited by St Patrick

The monks' fishing hut

Within the area are hundreds of islands, supported by thousands of rocks, shoals and shallows.

Each year some five thousand brown trout are caught in the mayfly season alone, while countless more are taken by trolling, the season starting on 15 February and ending on 30 September, with both wet fly and the dap in action in good conditions. And here again the experiences of Kingsmill Moore, who was an enthusiast for Corrib, are well worthwhile studying, not least because the two chapters, with his old boatman Jamsie who was a star in his own right, are not only good reading, but also a classic analysis of a fishery and how to fish it.

Perhaps it was his legal training that led him to examine with such care the lake's environment and food producing capacity, observing immediately the length of shore involved, thanks to the 'long and highly indented shore line,' with considerable extra length thanks to the islands. For where water meets land, particularly with the shallow nature of the lake and its high Ph levels, there will food most easily be created, led by snails and invertebrates of every shape and form. In these circumstances fat trout must thrive, as also will those cousins the ferox-cannibals who live deep and grab any small fish foolish enough to stray into their path, led by juvenile perch.

A typical Corrib troller

The judge fished, back in the 1930s, with a ten foot rod, casting twenty yards of line to perform what he called 'the long draw' – being exactly the basic method I use myself for all forms of boat fishing, be it for brown or rainbow trout, or salmon and sea trout. To vary the style employed is easy to do – the bob fly higher or the line sunk or a variation of speed in the recovery – but to have a longish line on the water for some time gives fish lying some way off, or deep down, a chance to reach a fly before it is cast again, something which the short line practitioners do not offer.

Jamsie however, whose absolutely different style of fishing was forced on him by entirely different equipment, fished in a manner that had been typical for a hundred years. The dominating factor was the line which was extremely light, and not tapered but level, something that could hardly be cast any distance and in no way in the style we now take as normal. To use it effectively, therefore, a long rod was essential, Jamsie's being some thirteen foot, and I quote.

The long rod and light line enabled the flies to be played on the surface at a sufficient distance from the boat in a variety of attractive ways, and even when the modern dressed line and shorter stiffer rod were introduced a number of good fishermen preferred to stick to the old methods in a modified form. At the end of his line the flies responded, sliding and circling, bobbing about like egg-laying spinners . . . like a windswept daddy,

This raises all sorts of thoughts, which suggest to me that we may have gone too far in the 'modern' direction. If in those days Jamsie could match the judge in numbers of fish netted by employment of some sort of cross between normal wet fly action and dapping, are we sure that something of value has not been lost? What is more, given today's quite incredibly light materials, a thirteen foot single-handed rod becomes an entirely different proposition, and when employed with a really light line almost exactly what Jamsie used, producing fish after fish. Why should this not work just as well today, its re-introduction with luck doing something to halt the almost universal trolling that one now sees, except in the mayfly season. While the judge talked about trolling early in the season for salmon, and for ferox, he records only fishing a fly himself, and much of his time there was in late summer, which can be hard work indeed.

When the salmon pass through the Galway fishery it is only a short distance to their first potential spawning river, the Clare River, entering the Lower Lake in the extreme south-east corner. It is the largest of Corrib's rivers, nearly sixty miles in length, making in the absence of hills somewhat sedate progress as it drains the plains of East Galway. It is far from famous as a salmon river, possibly because of its lowland surroundings, which I suspect as one who has only looked at and read about, but not fished it, may be a considerable misjudgement. For the Clare is the prime destination for the system's spring fish, followed by plenty of grilse, its limestone waters an ideal smolt producing environment. If and when the numbers of spring fish return to something like the old level, a visit in March or April should be an exciting proposition. Meanwhile the river also holds superb trout in large numbers.

Back at the lake early season trolling in the area of the Clare's entry produces fish, as does the bottom of the river itself above the weir.

The Narrows includes a mass of small islands and rocks and is primarily trout fishing, but at Oughterard the Oughterard or Owenriff River enters from the west, a spate river draining the hills around Maam Cross with a good grilse run, and some salmon, from July on. It has three loughs, Lead Mine Lake of just ten acres, Agraffard a bit larger and Bofin the largest at the top, all of which get a run not only of salmon and grilse, but also of large Corrib brown trout from August onwards as they move towards their spawning grounds. Combine these waters with the chances of a grilse in Oughterard Bay and this area has real attractions for the salmon lake angler.

Typical Corrib shoreline

A Corrib harbour – one of many

Elsewhere in The Narrows there are a mass of islands and shoals, where a good fisherman suitably guided by a local boatman will find brown trout for the taking, together with salmon lies to work. But success will reflect the expertise of your boatman and so will your safety, for rocks and reefs can be all over the place.

A good story told by the famous broadcaster of *Call My Bluff* fame, Paddy Campbell, relates to this area of the lake. A fisherman, late in the evening and well out from the shore, hooked a truly large trout which managed to swim through a gap in a shallow reef – the boat thereby the wrong side. The angler, not willing to lose his only fish of the day, got out into just six inches of water and in due course had his quarry in the net, turning to re-embark only to see his boat floating away on the gentle breeze. Short of a half mile swim – and he was not as young as he had been – there was no way he could reach the shore and he resolved to spend the night where he was, confident of rescue as fishermen set forth in the morning from the neighbouring harbour to the east.

However, it so happened that there was an excellent pub right by the harbour, so good that, from time to time, it attracted custom from the population resident on the west bank of The Narrows, some of whom that evening had made the crossing to celebrate a birthday. Thus it was that in the almost dark of early night the revellers – five of them – were rowing their way home, their passage designed to slip safely past the shallows well out in the lake, when the man in the stern leapt to his feet, crossed himself and burst into prayer begging the Almighty for mercy and forgiveness – adding he would never touch a Guinness again in his life!

His amazed companions, who as oarsmen were facing the other way, concluded that it must have been one too many he had indeed had, but turned to see what he was pointing at. For there walking on the water towards them was the son of God in person, come back to save sinners!

Chaos ensued for five minutes before it struck the boat party that some of the language being employed by the Deity himself had slipped a long way from the correct, with in particular his vivid description of how his ****** feet felt after an hour in the lake, and why would they not bring their bloody boat quickly to pick him up!

I met the narrator of this tale once and asked if it was true, and if so was it himself that had turned the Corrib into Galilee! To which the answer was yes and no – but I'll never be sure he wasn't pulling my leg!

The Middle Lake, the largest section in terms of acreage has two remarkably good hotels, just about as different from each other as it is possible to imagine, they are the Carrarevagh Hotel on the west side, a few miles north of Oughterard, and the Ashford Castle Hotel at Cong, mentioned before in connection with Noel Huggard, and previously a Guinness family mansion. The former is a little changed, typically Irish country house, its contents including pictures and furniture, plus tiger skin on the wall facing you in the hall, dating from about 1900 but with new plumbing, while the latter is massive, much modernised, hyper comfortable and in the best of taste up to date – marble bathrooms in the suites. The one is run by the owner, Harry Hodson, and his wife – who is a very remarkable chef at that – in a house his family has owned for five generations and the other has a team of highly trained executives and staff, the two catering for entirely different markets, and both doing a first class job.

At Carrarevagh I had a brief chat with their old head boatman Pat Mallow who knew Jamsie and who confirmed more or less what I already knew which was that the trout fishing, and particularly the mayfly, was if anything improving, but outside that period the fishing effort with a fly was diminishing, as trolling increased. He said that almost no deliberate fly fishing for salmon now took place, but some took a trout fisherman's fly by chance, although a French party had caught a few fish in the bay at the mouth of the Carrarevagh River, one of their spawning streams. And that makes one wonder how many more similar situations may exist, apart from the large feeder rivers. While in many cases salmon in such waters – and lake trout too – may be over ripe and should not be fished for, in the lake they should mainly be fair game for the angler, and two Middle Lake rivers that come to mind here being the Cornamona and Black Rivers.

The Cong River at Ashford

Up at Cong, thanks probably to a major hatchery operation, large numbers of salmon are caught in the short stretch of river between the lake and its re-emergence from below ground, having drained Loughs Mask and Carra, but at the river mouth the pressure looks to me a bit heavy, the fishing being free and all methods allowed. Nobody seems to know the numbers taken, but up to a thousand fish a year was put forward as likely, starting with a good spring run.

The hotel is a big draw for the American tourist trade, something which seems to limit the demand for fishing. That said Frank Costello who has an excellent boat hire business, more or less in the hotel grounds, covers any demand, following in his father's footsteps, being available also to non-hotel visitors.

The river looks delightful fishing for both fly and spinner, although if it were opened up with the trees suitably pruned it would be a great improvement, and if made fly-only that much better.

Lastly the Upper Lake which by the standards of the Corrib is quite small, looks to me to have real possibilities as a salmon fly fishery, but as ever expert local knowledge is essential if you are to find their lies. With two almost identical rocky points, for no obvious reason one will be favoured while the other is ignored. It is well known that this can happen on famous salmon rivers without any explanation, but it is even more likely to occur in lakes where the density of fish is so much lower.

Frank Costello and a 10lb trout

Joyce's River – spawning gravels

North-west Corrib

While some serious study of Peter O'Reilly's detailed comments on what is where on Corrib is a great help, a good local boatman must be the answer.

Although fishing Joyce's River is not encouraged late in the season, to protect both coloured salmon and lake trout due to spawn, I can't help feeling that given high water in June a cast in some of the best looking pools might well produce results, for salmon are quite capable of entering a river only to drop back to the lake if it gets too low.

One could spend one's life fishing the Corrib and never do more than know most of it quite well, having real familiarity with a few segments. That it offers a wide variety of extremely good and attractive fishing is certainly true and the only possible criticism that I can think of is that there are no sea trout. But if you wanted the cousins that went away to sea, Connemara and Mayo next door used to take care of that, and with luck will do so again before long.

Meanwhile this is a great fly fishery, may it remain just that, and if Jamsie could catch what he did with his long rod and feather light line, you can bet with practice it could be done again today.

Chapter 12

Mayo

I once in an article raised the question of where in Ireland should the truly all-round game fisherman go to retire, but concluded that for me it was just about impossible to choose between Waterville and Newport, and I am no further on to this day. Certainly in terms of salmon and sea trout, the two areas offer a mass of fishing – Waterville's sea trout larger but Newport having an incredible number of varied fisheries within an hour's drive. And these include the Moy River, with Loughs Conn and Cullin as feeders together with, going south, Delphi and the Erriff River, most of Connemara, Loughs Mask and Carra, and northern Corrib, plus a whole mass of less famous names, while to the north are the Burrishoole loughs and Carrowmore. Against that in County Kerry within an hour of Waterville there are also numerous alternative fisheries. Here, however, while a host of excellent migratory fisheries can be reached in that hour – the Glencar system to start with, the Laune beyond, and the little Blackwater River to the east – the brilliance of the brown trout fishing available around Newport may turn the scales in favour of a County Mayo base.

Certainly as we work up the coast from the south, passing through Connemara we can do little more than be excited by the prospects that emerge as we look at the mass of fishing that lies ahead. Starting at Delphi and the Erriff River, it goes on and on through Newport and Lough Beltra, to Burrishoole, then Carrowmore, and then the Moy River – perhaps Ireland's most productive and viable fishery system today, collectively attracting visiting anglers by the thousand. In the region both loughs and rivers offer fly fishermen sport of the highest quality, while those attached to a spinner or bait will find plenty of room too. In this personal taste takes over, but the thing that must be right is to have fish in the water to catch – and here they surely do!

There are great varieties to be found in Mayo's fisheries, something for all tastes, including – being so different from each other – very public and very private fisheries. And it is exactly that which is so fascinating, with regulars coming back year after year, knowing they have found what they want, hardly ever let down, extremes of weather being the only danger.

Essential to all this is the Government policy which gives real support to fisheries, plus Euro funds to help. The Burrishoole research effort is a typical example of that support, together with the regional boards at Galway and Ballina, actively engaged in improvement work. That visiting anglers contribute seriously to the local economy is fully understood, as is the fact that the quality of the fishing is important.

Go to Mayo with your rod, any time between April and October, and somewhere you will find some great fishing – salmon or sea trout or brown trout!

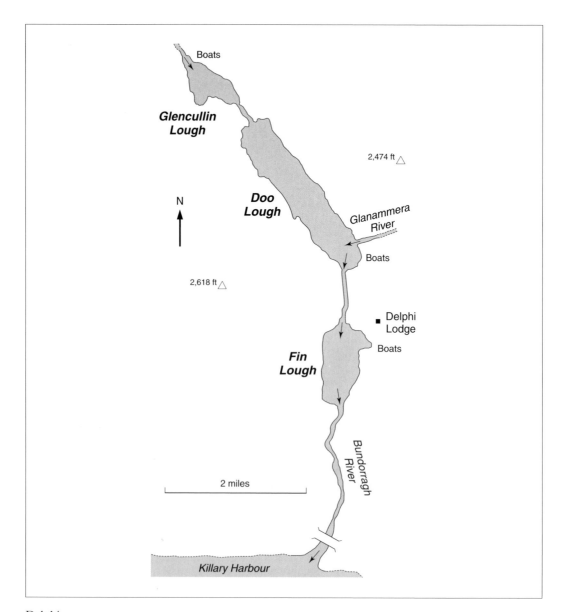

Delphi

Chapter 13

Delphi

If you approach Delphi by the usual route you will be coming either from Westport or Galway, therefore basically from the east, including with the latter some of the route we covered on our way to Ballynahinch. In which event to reach Delphi you must cross the Erriff River at the head of Killary Harbour, right next to the spectacular Aasleagh Falls, a natural dam-shaped rock formation which in flood is a miniature Niagara. With a sizeable fish pass at one side both salmon and sea trout have no trouble getting up river, which is much influenced by rain, there being only one lough, Tawnyard, in the system, in its day a first-class sea trout fishery.

High water, Aasleagh Falls – right by the sea

The tourist promoters are now calling Killary Harbour 'Ireland's only Fjord' with boat trips available, some eight miles down to the open sea, salmon and shellfish cage farms anchored in its narrow seaway.

In our case we go on down the right, the Mayo, shore of this curious narrow estuary for a few miles, and half way to the open ocean cross a bridge over a much smaller river, the Bundorragha, or Delphi, River. Running inland, its path followed loyally by the road towards a cleft between the massive Mweelrea Mountains on the left and Ben Gorm to the right, this is the country we saw so clearly on our way to Ballynahinch, the final home of the golden eagle in Ireland.

As you go up into the glen for the first time, you feel you should be holding your breath – your only companion the little river of rocky falls and pools scrambling up the gradient to the right – the mountains increasingly towering forbiddingly towards you, with ahead some sort of a pass within which, by some magic means, the road must find its way through the massif. Then quietly the valley flattens a little revealing a small lough and trees, and beyond the lake is a beautiful Georgian house – Delphi Lodge – comfortably sitting below the mountains facing south, in no way physically dominated, confident and clearly its own master, calling guests to its doorstep.

And at this point the educated reader is entitled to say 'hang on a minute, Delphi is in Greece, on the north side of the Bay of Corinth, this is south-west County Mayo – what's the link?' And you may also enquire reasonably why does the Irish west – particularly this area – go in for names that are utterly unexpected in their foreignness? For instance, ten miles from Delphi is the little coastal town of Louisburgh, which sounds like Germany to me, with just a few miles to its south the Carrowniskey River which should reasonably be Russian or Polish. Similarly not far from Waterville, where we began our journey, one finds Valentia Island – famous for its gale warnings – which surely must be Spanish, and indeed Spain is next stop over the Bay of Biscay – and lastly what about Costello which is as Italian as spaghetti!

To which the answer is that, for the latter four curiosities I have failed to unearth a reason, although someone said Valentia was connected with an Armada ship wrecked there on its way home. However against that the name Delphi was the inspiration of a gentleman named Browne, the 2nd Marquess of Sligo whose great house at Westport, some twenty miles north is very well worth a visit – the perfect Irish Georgian mansion that is not too huge, with the grandeur and grounds to go with it.

On Delphi's history, and the development of the fishery, one again finds our friend the judge, T.C. Kingsmill Moore, in *A Man May Fish* full of information. He records how the 2nd Marquess in the early nineteenth century, lived for a time and fell in love with Greece but was obliged by affairs to return, and had built on his massive estate a remote sporting lodge, which he called Delphi, although even an obliging impressionist artist would be hard pressed to record anything remotely resembling those sun baked Mediterranean mountain slopes of historic fame. But what a gesture!

Over the years the house was let to fishing parties and families for holidays, although being incredibly remote it was bypassed by the more normal fishing fraternity, until the house was starting to fall down. Its saviour was a scholarly Dublin accountant, Alec Wallace, who first took the fishing for a hotel he had constructed from an old country house near Louisburgh, followed by a long lease on Delphi Lodge to which he transferred operations having more or less rebuilt it. He ran what in fact were his hotels as a private country house party, there being no bar, but a book to record your drinks, and one large dining table where you sat down next to whoever was there, which great tradition continues with Peter Mantle to this day.

The judge came to Delphi quite late in life, so that the second edition of his book had to have a chapter added, which highlights the stark differences in fishing terms between his Costello and Fermoy experiences, and the very different Delphi environment. He also has some prize comments on those who came to fish at Delphi when he was there, the vast majority a mix of well educated members of the professions, often like Alec of real scholastic standing. Only a few failed to fit, and one hears the judicial syllables echo loud and clear:

> There was the odd pebble – two young guards officers who tried to throw around their very inconsiderable weight and a woman whose aggressive self-assurance was only matched by her ignorance – but these were swallows of only one season and when they applied for future bookings Alec was always unaccountably full up.

The Delphi fishery was one of the finest sea trout fisheries in Ireland, being converted by Peter Mantle to become a first-class salmon fishery when the sea lice killed off the trout. It has a catchment of twenty square miles – including huge areas of nearly naked rock in the mountains – with four loughs and the short river up from the sea.

At the top end of the system the remote Lough Cunnell is of little importance as a fishing water having only small brown trout as residents, draining into the top end of Lough Glencullin. This is a smallish lough, with easy access – a feature of all Delphi's fishings – and has a capacity for two boats and once was an excellent white trout venue, producing also the odd salmon. Being so high in the system it fishes best later in the season.

A short step down the connecting stream one is at the head of Doo Lough (the dark lake) over two miles long, up to half a mile wide, most of it seriously deep, and reminding me of Loch Hope in the extreme north-west corner of Scotland. There it is the towering Ben Hope 3040 ft (927m) that dominates, here it is the mass of Mweelrea, up to 2618 ft (819m) to the south that leans over the loughside to darken the water you ride on. Nor should you imagine that the other loughside is much more open, for the Sheeffry Hills crowd in on you from the east. This is almost a huge gorge and no place to find yourself unprepared in a gale or storm for, exactly as we discovered at Waterville on Derriana the day the Zulu won first prize, waterspouts occur in certain circumstances, and a big one will sink you.

Doo Lough – first view from the west

At the bottom of the lake, a short river runs steeply for a few hundred yards through open woodland into the bottom lough of the system. Before you realise what is happening, the whole ambience has changed – behind you dark waters, the black rocks of the mountainside and then suddenly it is an open bowl of sunshine with the warmth of a different climate. And there lies Fin Lough – being in Gaelic the fair lake – with the lodge on its shores and relatively shallow and somewhere you would have to catch fish. And that, together with the river, is exactly what the visiting anglers do in very large numbers, landing salmon, with far fewer trout these days, the result of an emergency programme forced on Peter Mantle in 1990, his sea trout catch having fallen from an average of around 2000 in the 1960s/70s to a few hundred of largely juvenile fish. Clearly the sea trout were no longer Delphi's great attraction and something had to be done urgently. Could they convert to salmon? It was risky but possible, and with great courage that is what happened, using the ranching method whereby smolts are reared in hatcheries, being fed for a year prior to release as migrants to the ocean.

Great credit is due to Peter Mantle, and his backers, and the Irish authorities who helped and encouraged him to keep a great legend alive. As a result the fishery and hotel contribute annually some £400,000 a year to a largely destitute wilderness economy.

Fin Lough – river entry and a different climate!

Fin Lough – much too calm

Today the vast majority of salmon are taken from Fin Lough and the river below it, since almost none of the ranched fish go beyond their point of smolt release, which is the stream immediately above Fin Lough, adjacent to the hatchery. Indeed in the record year when a total of 1043 fish were landed, only seventy-one were taken above Fin Lough, with sixty-six in Doo Lough and five in Glencullin, while below, the river produced 470 and Fin Lough 502, a staggering catch for so small an area of water, the lake's last five years averaging about 250.

Most of this remarkable little lough can be fished, with after a spate fairly obviously the point of river entry a choice spot, and I can think of few places where, in a soft south-west wind in late June your chances should be better. For myself I would opt for an 11 foot rod, No. 5 line floater, but also having a slow sinker available on a second rod, in case it got cold or they wouldn't come up to the surface. I would use quite small flies – sizes 10 and 12 – in such conditions, and a Black Pennel, Claret Bumble, Bibio, Watson's Fancy or a Silver Stoat would keep me happy, going bigger if the wind got up and it rained, the same for both salmon and sea trout.

Glencullin – the top Delphi lake

On Glencullin a good sea trout

Briefly in the boat – 3½lb and fresh

On Doo Lough my approach would be quite different, as would my style of fishing, for here my 12 foot Charles McLaren should be perfect, with its old No. 5 floater, that just sinks at the tip. My flies also, for the dark lake, would be larger for both species, using most of the time size 8, with the bob fly heavily dressed, to include Black Pennel, Daddy, Zulu, Claret Bumble, and for the tail obviously a Delphi Silver, Silver Stoat, Hairy Mary or perhaps that Peter Ross, with in a wind a double hook to improve the 'anchorage' needed to work the bob correctly. Here too I would have a second rod with a slow sinker, being prepared to cast a long line to retrieve fast, that as I explain later will give me the maximum flexibility for variable fly presentation, which I find essential. Put crudely with a 12 foot rod one can almost be dapping, thanks to its light line, while at the other extreme for salmon, possibly using my other 12 foot heavier rod, with a heavy tube fly, or perhaps a small shrimp treble, on the tail you can get down deep if for whatever reason that seems the answer, all options between being open.

Two further and important points to make are first that the techniques needed for early spring fishing, and the flies suitable then, will vary considerably from summer methods. Then flies will be larger – a Collie Dog tube being popular up to 3 inches length – the speed of recovery slower and more deliberate, both on lough and river.

Secondly, when after salmon and big sea trout, due to its depth, the method of fishing Doo Lough is restricted largely to the two shore drifts, for the fish lie remarkably close to rocky features, visible as points or sometimes just below the surface. And it is here your boatman really earns his money, their team led by David McEvoy fishery manager and first class angler!

A number of points arise regarding the remarkable success of the Delphi ranching project – rearing smolts to go to sea – that may be of interest. The first is the very obvious question: if it is possible to create a salmon fishery in this manner, then why are more similar schemes not put in hand elsewhere? To which the basic answer is cost, for the rearing of smolts is expensive in both initial capital outlay and operation, typically when starting from scratch, £3 and £1 per smolt respectively. Thus at Delphi, set up to send 50,000 smolts to sea a year, having spent £150,000 on the hatchery, you then have two years' operating expense before a single adult salmon, a grilse, returns.

Meanwhile since fish reared in such artificial conditions are less able to cope in the wild, the oceanic survival level will be low, and in western Ireland, with the offshore drift nets, unlikely to be more than four per cent. Thus with 2000 adults returning – and capital costs written off over five years – each smolt therefore costing £1.60, every ranched adult in turn will have involved £40 for the first five years and £25 each thereafter. With a twenty per cent catch rate 400 will be taken by anglers, to which add say an average of 100 wild fish – all released – and it becomes very clear that on a stand alone basis salmon ranching is a long way from being a money maker, the presence of a hotel vital if ends are ever to meet.

Actual results, 1992 to 2000, show the wild salmon average as 115 fish out of a total of 455. The best year was 1998 with a 1043 total and the worst (excluding the start up year of 1992) 217 in the drought of 1996, although 1999 was almost as bad for the same reason and 229 was the total. While lack of water is always a problem with small rivers, when one has drift nets on one's doorstep in a confined space, which in the 2000 season took 3000 salmon in eight weeks – half Delphi and half Erriff fish – the problem is acute.

Another interesting factor at Delphi is the strain of fish now employed with comparative trials put in hand before the project started. They used smolts reared from their own local Bundorragha salmon, the Cong hatchery on Corrib, and Burrishoole, Salmon Research Agency fish and all were released simultaneously. All returning adults were captured, which with tagging meant accurate identification, the Burrishoole fish winning comfortably. This was logical since the latter were line-bred ranching fish, going back to 1952 when the Burrishoole project was started. With selective breeding using returning adults, oceanic survival seems to improve as the years go by, while the numbers of wild fish caught, if anything, also seems to get better.

This trend may also apply to sea trout as I was able to prove myself on my recent trip, for which my limited efforts were well rewarded as my diary shows:

28 August Glencullin 3 to 6pm. 3ST, best 3½lb, all to Daddy, others 1lb. Little wind – fair day.

30 August Glencullin 4 to 7pm. 6 ST to 1½lb. NW gale, fished from bank, Daddy and Raven No. 10

31 August Fin Lough Morning – ST – lost good salmon – plenty of fish!

Doo Lough Afternoon – 9 ST to 1½lb. Sunny with cloud, SW wind, and lots of trout!

While to lose a good salmon is infuriating always, this was clearly no small grilse but a fish that responded to a large Sedge on the bob, taking the Raven 10 double on the tail coming fast towards the boat – the hook came back after ten seconds! I was fishing with Mike Lydon, one of the hatchery team and an excellent fisherman, who is a noticeably quiet sort of a man, who much to my surprise exploded with a shouted oath at this disaster! He was right, for August needs a morale booster from time to time to keep the troops happy!

Michael – Fin Lough 1¼lb sea trout

In the net

The Delphi Silver did me well but most of the sea trout came to my Daddy or Mike's Green Peter also cutting the surface. After the dire shortages in recent years, plus the news from Ballynahinch, is this really the turning point for sea trout – and why? To which the answer may be the food being used in the salmon cages that contains an anti-louse element. Long may it last.

Below Fin Lough the river itself has huge charms, nearly all of it fast flowing, pool after pool with white water at their head offering ideal lies for fresh fish, and to the angler a target for his fly. A single-handed rod will suffice, but in my view the longer the better, while for spring with heavy flies employed, my 12 foot rods would work well. It must also be remembered that the angler should take great care not to stand on top of the fish, but if possible keep back from the bank – the longer the rod the easier this is to achieve. I have only caught small sea trout in the river, but a big fish in high water one would not forget in a hurry!

River Erriff – spate running off

It would be wrong to leave this special little area without some mention of the Erriff river we crossed on our way to Delphi. As I said it is mainly a spate river but even in low water it is fishable, for there are plenty of fast runs at the head of a series of pools. Nor should one ignore the long slow stretches, provided there is a reasonable, preferably upstream, wind to give the surface a ripple. The old Scottish method of 'backing-up' also works well here, as it should.

There are almost no spring fish – far fewer than at Delphi – and most of the time it is fly only something that for me would require no enforcement, but I would want my 12 foot rod handy for high water when a 2 inch tube with a sinking line might prove handy. I have fished it twice, always expecting but failing to get a fish, but in not very promising conditions. It is perfect fly water, the banks well cared for by the Central Fisheries Board who own it.

You can stay at Aasleagh Lodge or the Cottage, there are ten beats with about fifty named pools, as well as Lough Tawnyard, so that in good water there is plenty of room, the total capacity being twenty-two rods. Around 500 to 600 fish are caught each year, today the majority grilse, although the river has a run of summer salmon, and a huge fish of 45lb was once caught on fly by the then leasee of the river in the 1960s, a Mrs Dodds-Marsh.

This can be a very good river indeed, mountains all round you, and not a place easy to forget – like its neighbour Delphi.

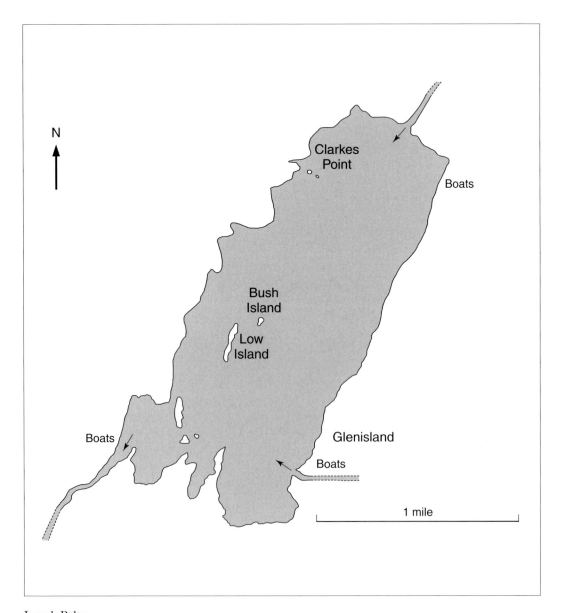

N

Clarkes
Point

Boats

Bush
Island

Low
Island

Glenisland

Boats

Boats

1 mile

Lough Beltra

Chapter 14

Lough Beltra

When we moved up from Kerry to Connemara it was a day's travel, made longer by our diversions certainly, but we went from one part of Ireland to another, and had a good look at the country on our two hundred mile trip – just 120 miles over the sea direct as the eider flies. From Delphi to Newport, even by the scenic route – requires at maximum two hours. In fact as the raven flies – for this is far from eider country – it is only twenty miles from one beautiful Georgian building to the next, Delphi Lodge to the Newport House Hotel. And to get there one can take three routes.

First, the obvious one and that is to retrace our steps alongside the Erriff River, turn left and follow the river and main road up the valley into the hills and on north to Westport. Secondly, one can go up the side of Doo Lough, past Glencullin, and keep going until one reaches the ocean at Louisburgh, turning right along the south shore of Clew Bay, to pass just north of Croagh Patrick. The holy mountain is 2310ft (705m) and its symmetrical peak looks massive. An almost perfect pyramid seen from the east, it is visible from fifty miles as you head for the west through Castlebar. Then third, at the bottom end of Doo Lough you could turn right on not much more than a track, an old mountain road running up the line of another Delphi spawning water, the Glenamerra River, a big stream leading east, offering good gravels for autumn fish, then past a tributary of the Erriff that drains what once was a great white trout lough, Tawnyard. Clinging to hillsides you wander through truly wild country whose streams also feed the upper Erriff, and emerge a few miles short of Westport on the Leenane road.

Each of these routes has its merit and for the geologist there is great interest as we shall see. But first a word about the holy mountain where Ireland's patron saint spent forty days and forty nights in emulation of Our Lord, as penance for the people of Ireland. It was in the fifth century at a time when the ancient Celtic church was growing fast, in the end embracing Brittany, through Cornwall to Wales, to Ireland, back to Iona in the Hebrides to Northumberland, Holy Island and Durham – a splinter of the true cross, solid in its unique faith. But not for long, as St Augustine appeared in Canterbury, sent by the Pope, the two sides coming face to face at the Synod of Whitby that dragged on for the summer of AD 664. The argument was won in the end by the newcomers, claiming written evidence from the hand of St Peter in person, stating that theirs was the only true faith, and all others were heretical – therefore the Celtic church must reform and accept the demands of Rome or be excommunicated!

Faced with disaster, and to him blasphemy, recorded by the Venerable Bede, the

Beltra from the east side

Bishop of Durham, Colman, leader of the old church refused to accept defeat, packed his bags and, together with a number of his most trusted and devout clergy, left for Ireland, and in particular Clare Island in Clew Bay. Here, in isolation and sanctuary, every morning the sun would rise over the shoulder of Croagh Patrick, and here without the influence of Rome, literally in the shadow of his mountain, carrying the footprints of Ireland's first great saint they would end their lives unmolested. How many subsequent hermits in their beehive huts were inspired by this example is impossible to guess, while it is not for nothing that Whitby's name has become familiar to schoolboys, for that transfer of power was of great significance. In fact the status quo was maintained for nine hundred years until broken by Henry VIII in 1536, for reasons that were linked precisely to power and wealth, being well recorded. An interesting question therefore arises as to which side would St Patrick have been on at Whitby? And you can think about that on a quiet drift across Lough Beltra or Furnace, for Croagh Patrick is just a few miles over the sea in full view. Upon which issue you may conclude that today it hardly matters, while the saint very probably, like so many early supporters of Christianity, would have been a handy catcher of fish too, and on Beltra would have known the best salmon lies blindfolded!

On our journey, for me anyway, this unusual spiritual influence starts to be felt the moment the gradient changes beyond Doo Lough to downhill towards Louisburgh, the top of the Carrowniskey River beside us and then lower down the Bunowen River, both producers of salmon in numbers after a good spate. From here the view with Clare Island half left is over the bay towards Achill Island with its great cliffs dropping over 2000ft (730m) straight into the ocean. To the right are a sprinkling of small islands at the head of the bay, with both Westport and Newport beyond, and we decide to have a look at the Sligo family seat as we pass through the former – finding it just as impressive as suggested by our earlier remarks, the classic Irish mansion.

But suddenly this is quite flat lush country for the few miles to Newport, the little town set comfortably both sides of the Newport River estuary, right at the top of the tide with two handsome grey stone bridges. And rather as at Waterville, you come on

The Newport River – often forgotten

this picture suddenly, particularly from the south, with from that side facing you immediately over the water at high tide, the Newport House Hotel, its front covered with virginia creeper, with a long waterfront, fine beech trees, lawns and shrubs. It is over the bridge, through the gates first left, with inside the house high ceilings, huge rectangular windows, with glass panes of a size that match, the classic Georgian dimensions and much loved by Prince Ranier and Princess Grace of Monaco who were regular visitors in their day. This is five stars in spades, with – thanks to Kieran Thompson who owns the hotel – a menu to match, supported by a wine cellar that would be described as brilliant in a Loire chateau. And consequently you will not find it so easy to do much sea trout fishing after dinner, although night fishing on the Newport River was at one time first class, as I proved.

Meanwhile for the inquiring angler, how about that geology I keep going on about? For surely there must be a massive change from the peat and rock environment of Delphi, to which the answer is very much yes, and needless to say somewhat complex. On our route, starting in a big block of ancient ordovician, on

Newport – the upper river

the way to Louisburgh it changes to the slightly younger silurian, then through a small strip of old red sandstone – Croagh Patrick itself being ancient igneous volcanic basalt – then to those younger rocks, correctly in terms of the geological timetable, an extension of the carboniferous limestones that cover most of central Ireland and which we found at Corrib. Somehow a strip of this best fish rearing rock available had squeezed its way down from Lough Conn between twin ridges of old red sandstone to embrace most of Clew Bay, and within it lie Loughs Beltra, Furnace and Feagh. These waters we shall therefore visit with high hopes, knowing that against some less favoured environments, juvenile fish here will have had a head start in life, which for the angler means confidence from day one.

Also in this region we shall be going with equal confidence on to Bangor, thirty miles north, to fish Lough Carrowmore, a quite large but shallow lake, that many today believe to be the best salmon lough in Ireland. What a prospect it all is!

Sometimes it is particularly annoying to lose one's fishing notes, sometimes it doesn't matter a hoot. Unfortunately my first visit to Ireland's west coast in July 1965, hoping to catch sea trout, falls into the former category. We had two non-fishing days – one out at sea from Achill Sound, one playing golf and having a look around, and with reasonable weather it was great fun. We fished Loughs Beltra, Feagh and Furnace, and I did some night fishing on the river, my own competence as a lough fisherman developing rapidly, not least by observing the techniques employed by the old hands present, some annual regulars with years of experience behind them.

My family and I stayed at Newport House Hotel, then as today extremely comfortable, and owned and managed by the then current generation of the Mumford-Smith family, supported by a superb major domo called Owen. He was a cross between butler, tourist guide, adviser on where the boys should fish, an expert on where to shop and for what, what was special for dinner that night, which flies to use on the river (as against the loughs) etc, etc! It turned out that he was almost as famous in the hotel fishing world of Ireland as Noel Huggard, and a completely exceptional man, who sadly died quite young. One curiosity occurred when he sent my wife into Newport to a tailor who as he worked sat cross-legged on a table, stitching away by hand – straight out of Dickens – and when asked why he sat on a table rather than a chair Owen answered, 'where else would a tailor sit?'

I mentioned the holidays taken in Newport by Princess Grace of Monaco, previously Grace Kelly, the famous film star having an American/Irish lineage, the family coming from just outside Newport. In fact the ancestral homestead is right beside Drumgoney Lough – local name thanks to its shape the Leg of Mutton Lake – to the right of the Newport to Castlebar road. While it may all look fine and prosperous today with the country full of cattle and sheep, west Mayo was terribly hit by the potato blight famine a hundred and fifty years ago, with many forced to leave their farms, and many also heading for Boston.

Against Delphi's mountains, and the rocky moonscape of Connemara, to be in the fertile lushness of Newport with wild fuchsias flowering everywhere at the roadside, tropical plants in the gardens healthy and well, is a huge contrast. With the warm and moist Atlantic climate, one feels almost a lotus-eater, and the hotel's garden proved the point. It is therefore an unexpected transformation going inland up the river to Lough Beltra, to find as the valley opens out, that the lushness is very local, reflecting exactly the geological structures already mentioned. The limestone runs under the lowland of the valley stretching from the sea, on past Beltra, to spread wide at Lough Conn, with on each side parallel old red sandstone hills culminating in Nephim, on your left, rising out of the plain largely bare rock, a spectacularly massive dominating mountain of 2646ft (807m). Each side of the valley with heather on the open and wild moorland, the tops are well over 1000ft (305m) and good rain magnets, their environment utterly different to the fertile valley.

Lough Beltra therefore is a curious mixture of geological richness located in an area of more or less the reverse. This bastard arrangement clearly suits migratory fish very well, and is reflected by the output of the River Moy, draining Lough Conn ten miles on, which produces salmon in huge numbers, although here the spring run is relatively small. And it is the spring salmon of Beltra, for which it has earned such a great reputation, the season opening on 20th March with good results up to the end of May, and it could easily open earlier. It is a fly only lake, which may deter some anglers, with no noisy trolling to disturb the shallows and points where the fish lie. It was once also a great sea trout lake where during a subsequent visit with a day ticket on a July day, with my younger son we had fourteen averaging 1½lb, putting back another four, the largest 2½lb, but by then we had been busy on Currane and at Costello to brush up our technique. But an oddity that sticks in the mind on that first visit – when our best effort was eight trout in a day – included the curious discovery that a hatching mayfly I had put on the bob worked extremely well, while not a natural did we see once, although Conn just up the road enjoys a good hatch in late May and June.

Which only goes to confirm the view, discussed below, that the built in reaction by any form of 'hunter' on seeing a possible food item escaping, is to grab it quickly! The lure, therefore, needs only to be a plausible imitation of that 'possible food item' to work in this instance, and not a close replica of an actual creature. The best example of this latter point relates to Ian Wood, the great Loch Lomond angler who when afloat, used throughout the season while salmon fishing exactly the same fly pattern on both bob and tail, his invention bearing his name, with sizes 4 to 8 in the early spring, falling to 8 to 12 as the weather warmed up. While it is impossible to argue with his achievements, and his fishing methods also were similarly unvaried – long rod and short line only – for me half a dozen fly patterns, combined with differing fishing styles adds to the interest, and in my view also improves the chances of success.

In all of this, however, one does need to recognise that there are real differences

Lough Beltra – much wanted rain

between how to catch salmon and white trout. For the former, particularly in the early cold months when larger fish are about, the 'modus operandi' will be slower and more deliberate, with a slow reaction to the fly being taken if you want to avoid pulling the fly away from the fish before it has closed its mouth. Let him turn down, or away, and only tighten when he pulls you in a solid, rod bending manner. Later, with the grilse of summer, and even more so with the smaller white trout, much faster reactions are required, but even then try to judge the size and if possible type of fish – grilse or trout – in the split second available. Again the rule is to give the larger creatures more time, but judgment on this score is very far from easy, even with many years' experience!

Lough Beltra has one feature that is unusual for there is a notional line dividing the fishing rights more or less in half, from end to end. A total of ten boats may be fished at any one time with basically five each side. The Newport House Hotel has the western section and a local anglers' association, the Glenisland Co-operative in

Castlebar the eastern beat. Hotel residents obviously take precedence, having the river fishing as well, but boats when not in use may be hired from either organisation, making this first class fishery open to visiting anglers most of the time. There are however obvious and special circumstances – opening day for instance – which means heavy local demand.

The flies used, particularly in the early season tend to be rather more traditional and on the large side, with well known specifically salmon patterns popular, such as Silver Doctor, Thunder and Lightning or Hairy Mary, plus of course the Beltra Badger. Indeed I once heard of a good fish taken on a size 4 double prawn fly by a visiting Scandinavian! But, by Irish standards Beltra fish are larger than average, middle 'teens' of weight common, with from time to time a salmon over 20lb! The fisherman in the spring should therefore be prepared for a serious tussle: nylon leaders of 15lb, a powerful rod and a net in the boat that is big and strong! While for your summer grilse of 6 or 7lb, the use of 8lb nylon and a 10 foot rod is perfectly possible, but think again for the spring when I believe a 12 foot double handed rod has many advantages!

I mentioned the sea trout night fishing used to be first class, and so it was before the sea lice plague. For instance I once, on my first visit had with five casts three trout and then hooked a grilse which after five minutes got into a fallen branch and broke me. I was just above the Castlebar road bridge half a mile up from the town, the river having a series of little weirs with the pools above them made for white trout, fishing being easy from the field on the right bank. It was just after midnight and I had been at it for two hours with a couple of 1lb trout taken, not much going on, and time to head for my bed. But one more go, I thought, with a different fly might work, so I attached a little half inch shrimp tube fly, with plenty of jungle cock each side with the contrasting black and white clearly visible in the dark.

The first cast produced a better trout of 1¾lb, the second another rather smaller, the third was blank, the fourth another trout and the fifth the first salmon I ever hooked at night. And, you may ask, how do I know it was a salmon and not a very large white trout, to which I can only answer that although I cannot prove it, the reaction of the fish was utterly different, being almost sedate in its movements, while anyway to run into what must have been at least a 5lb trout at that time of year would be most unusual. Lastly I can add, having subsequently caught a Scottish salmon at night which acted in the same measured – in fact rather boring – manner, the performance was unlike any sea trout I ever hooked. But I was mighty sad at its loss!

Meanwhile the river today, while short of its own wild trout, has an entirely unexpected visitor to be encountered on occasion. Thanks to escapees from rearing cages in Clew Bay, rainbow trout appear from time to time, having all the characteristics of their American west coast parentage where the steelhead – the sea-run rainbow – is a prize to be sought. And do not kid yourself that these escapees are, thanks to a protected early life, some form of a soft touch, for quite the reverse is the case as I discovered on a recent visit. While Kieran Thompson had told me about their presence – and I had seen a good steelhead that was caught the day before – when I hooked what I believed was a quite decent spring salmon, below the weir where the road turns away from the river, which set off for the sea like a champion, I had no doubts about the nature of my catch. And it was only when I saw it in the net at only about 6lb – I had expected 10lb at least from its strength – that I woke up to the truth. So I now have fun telling my American fishing friends about my steelhead experience – in Ireland.

The weir pool – where the steelhead took

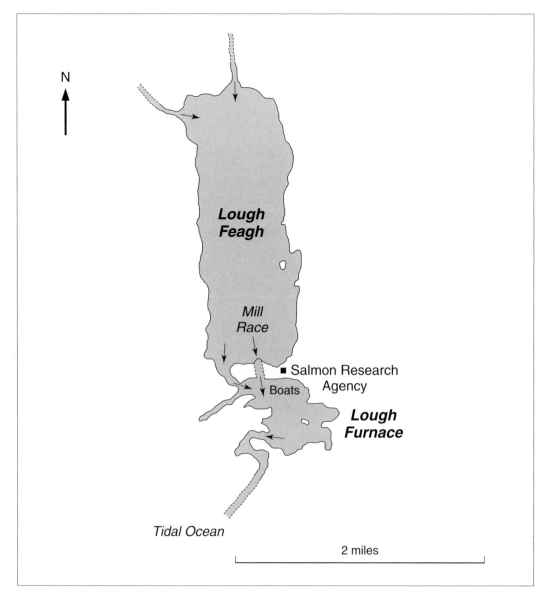

N

Lough
Feagh

Mill
Race

■ Salmon Research
Agency

Boats

Lough
Furnace

Tidal Ocean

2 miles

Burrishoole Fishery

Chapter 15

Furnace and Feagh

It was a dull nondescript sort of a fly, a very lightly dressed bumble with no wing or tail, and the orangey red segment half way down its black fur body immediately caught the eye, the wire ribbing extremely fine.

'I don't imagine you have anything quite like this in your box but I find it does well with the sea trout here. I call it the Bibio after a heather fly you find in these parts – it's black with a few red points.'

The speaker was Major Charles W. Roberts, on my very first day's Irish fishing, as we waited for the boatman by the little harbour on Lough Feagh. This was the owner and manager of the Burrishoole fishery, Lough Furnace being the complementary lower half with only a few yards between the two lakes, and his fly in 1969 was just emerging on a career that was to know no bounds, becoming a standard pattern for lakes, lochs, and reservoir anglers, and hugely popular. That said his original bore little relationship to the heavily dressed versions that are deemed correct today, which while excellent bumbles in their own right, are not what was then almost a lightly palmered nymph. The open body hackle's density was similar to that of a Soldier Palmer, while exactly as with a Royal Wolf or Coachman the central section was eye catching, and provided a sort of thorax impression. With sizes 10 and 12 I have caught hundreds of fish, including salmon and sea trout plus both brown and rainbows.

From the Newport House Hotel, Owen had packed us off that first day with the standard, and not small, picnic basket well stocked with cold meat, bread, butter and cheese, fruit cake and tea bags, with the advice that our man would make the tea. We didn't do very well, but after lunch I got a couple of sea trout of about 1¼lb each, very fresh and silver, while I saw several salmon showing. So began a very personal love affair with the loughs of western Ireland, which only in hopeless conditions have ever failed to produce some sort of result whenever I have fished them, with red letter days that stick in the mind to come back vividly many years later.

Charles Roberts had fought the war as a regular major in the British Royal Artillery, and with peace restored had returned to his family property – a house in the trees overlooking its Lough Feagh fishery. Lough Furnace was bought shortly afterwards, being then a run down salmon and sea trout fishery, which, in his absence, had been poached almost to extinction. The netting of Furnace that had once averaged 160 salmon and 600 grilse a year which he then owned was stopped, and he came up with the idea that with a stocking programme a new re-enhanced fishery might make some money, and help the area all round.

The river above Lough Feagh.

It also seemed to him that if he was going to be rearing salmon and white trout by a variety of means including sending smolts off to sea, it would be interesting to combine this improvement programme with basic research into things like oceanic survival rates and which sort of strain of fish did best or worst. What was more, thanks to the physical layout it was relatively easy to install an accurate counting mechanism that recorded all fish movements down from, or up into, Lough Feagh – smolts and kelts post spawning migrating, with mature adults returning from the sea. However, while a good idea, this needed a lot more money than he himself could lay his hands on, calling for help from a suitable, and wealthy, sponsor, which in Ireland in those days meant only one name – Guinness, who duly obliged.

So it was that 'The Salmon Research Trust of Ireland Incorporated' was formed in 1952, to become the leading research operation of its type in the British Isles, and well developed by the time I got there in 1969. Over the years the Irish Government became first a partner with those already involved and in the end took over the whole operation. It became 'The Salmon Research Agency', and they have carried on the very open attitude to the public, welcoming visiting fishermen to their doorstep, and never losing sight of the fact that their task of salmon stock improvement is primarily a service for anglers – since it is visiting fishermen who contribute so much to remote local economies. Their work on a wide range of salmonid subjects is now famous, some of their investigations taking many years to complete, a typical recent report – being highly relevant where escapee farmed fish are common – was a study of the impact which the introduction of fast growing non-indigenous juvenile salmon have on slower growing native strains. Needless to say the answer is what one would expect – bad for the natives – but the point was to prove it.

As a result of such research, and the fact that over the years the output of the hatchery, which is located between the two loughs, had grown massively, a major 'ranching' operation as the smolt release enhancement method is named, had emerged. However, in these circumstances management started to worry that the original natural and wild stocks would be physically swamped and subject to cross breeding. It was therefore decided that while Furnace, the lower lake, should be developed to the maximum as a ranched fishery with all wild fish being released, Feagh itself would be left as a reserve for wild fish only with no fishing allowed, its feeder streams being studied and ideal for various trials.

Since at the same time, exactly as with Beltra and the Newport River next door, the sea trout population had largely been wiped out, the position today is very different to that available to us on our first visit thirty-two years ago. But, and a very big but it is, Lough Furnace now is one of the finest grilse fisheries anywhere, starting in mid-June, and able to produce prolific sport to the season's end on 30 September, with four or five fish in a day quite possible for an experienced fisherman in good conditions. On which subject there is none more expert than Peter O'Reilly and I quote from his *Trout and Salmon Loughs of Ireland* 'Furnace is a lovely lough, with shallow bays that can turn up either a sea trout or a salmon and there is always somewhere to fish, no matter what point the wind is from.' And that latter characteristic for a salmon lough, be it in Ireland, north-west Scotland or the Hebrides is singularly rare, and of great value.

For both Peter and me, Furnace gave us our first lake salmon taken with a fly from a boat, mine with a Black Pennel, his with a Kenyaman, although my guess is that today he would pick a Green Peter as the fly most likely to succeed. It is a famous old trout sedge pattern and I quote again, 'It was on this lough that the Revd. Canon P.J. Gargan the Cavan priest and international fly fisherman first popularised the Green Peter as a fly for salmon'. In my experience fished on the bob quite fast cutting the surface it is as good as they come with one minor reservation, which is that I believe it is at its best in good light, whereas in overcast and dull conditions a Claret Bumble or Bibio (and Zulu in a black gale and rain as discussed) can have the edge. Exactly the same comment applies to another old friend, the Daddy, which on a bright day when plenty of naturals are being blown out over the water, can be mighty effective, as we saw at Delphi. Among other factors involved I have found are that, entirely logically, the brighter the light the smaller the fly should be – and salmon in lakes prefer small-sized flies – while the dressing itself should become similarly reduced. So, bearing in mind the old adage, 'dark day, dark fly – light day, light fly', combined with parallel fly size adjustment, having discovered what flies are doing well, you can put up your rod with real confidence. Show the salmon, and grilse in particular, a fly that is something like a juvenile food source – as suggested a sedge or daddy longlegs for instance that is about to escape and you may spark a reaction – to make a grab at it by instinct. The concept of the induced take is well known and employed on chalk streams with nymphs, but here it is the skated fly that does it!

Thus on Furnace, on a really good day in mid-summer, I would be hoping with two rods in a boat for half a dozen grilse, averaging 5lb, and even into double figures if they were taking properly, and not just splashing at the fly! Similarly in the old days Feagh had the same generous spirit, and Peter O'Reilly records 'It will always be one of my favourite loughs, and why not? It once turned up five salmon for me on an August afternoon – all on a Green Peter.'

Feagh also, one late September, gave an American friend of mine his first ever salmon on a Zulu, in a full gale from the south-east that kept us, for safety reasons, close to the shore adjacent to the harbour. I had a sea trout of about 3lb immediately and lost a salmon thanks to the nylon taking a turn round the hook of my Bibio on the dropper, something one cannot see while fishing! Twenty-five years later on Lough Carrowmore exactly the same thing happened, preventing me from having three 'springers' in one day, all on small flies – which would have been a personal record. It doesn't sound a great number, but these days with so few spring salmon, most of which tend to be taken on the troll, three in a day is a triumph.

It is a curiosity of nature that the Burrishoole lakes have no spring run when next door is Beltra, a famous spring salmon fishery, and Carrowmore just up the coast is the same. But as we saw, while Delphi has always had a spring run, its immediate

Lough Furnace – the Millrace.

neighbour the Erriff River only has a token spring salmon or two, for no obvious reason. This is made even more curious if one realises that when the Delphi salmon ranching project was launched, the stock selected after trials was Burrishoole, line bred, ranching stock, which produces at home no spring fish! However, with their new habitat and selective breeding, Peter Mantle is now reporting increasing numbers of ranched spring salmon at Delphi – the good early catches for 2001 being some seventy-five per cent from reared stocks, which is quite extraordinary.

What I had not expected, on my last visit, was to be told of a quite exceptional man, Sean Nixon, who had made a truly remarkable impact on the management of fisheries in the mid-western coastal district. Since I had known several managers of The Salmon Research Agency over the years, I was surprised that I had never heard the name, for his input as a strenuous guardian of salmon and sea trout, between the years 1949 and 1996 had been extraordinary – in both private and public employment. His so far unpublished autobiography, lent me by John Mulrany, a leader in the team at Galway, made it clear that no book that I was writing could be complete without meeting such a remarkable man, so we had a long chat in his house looking south over Clew Bay to Croagh Patrick.

He had dedicated his life to fishery improvement and his book is descriptively entitled, *Guarding the Silver the introduction of correct and proper management of migratory salmonids*.

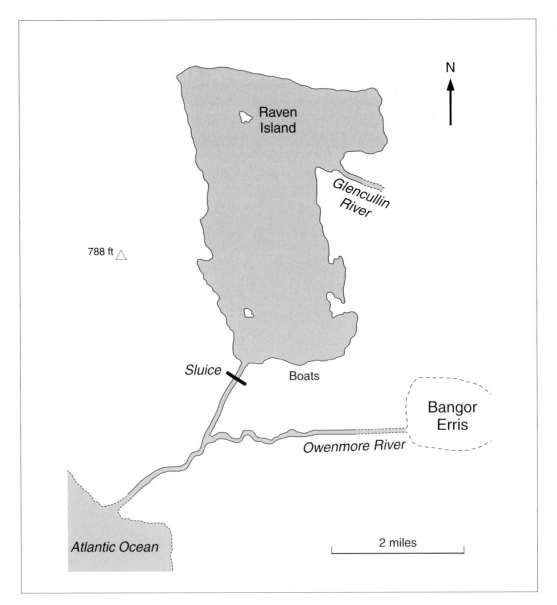

Lough Carrowmore

Chapter 16

Carrowmore

As is often the case when visiting somewhere new, one has a good look at the map of the region, and when on a fishing trip lakes and rivers obviously will catch the eye. By this means the presence of a large lough about thirty miles north-west of Newport led me to enquire, on my 1969 visit to Newport, if it was any good for sea trout, because it certainly looked particularly well placed. All, or almost all, loughs with access to the sea in that part of Ireland had runs of fish, with those large enough having salmon too, but here was a lough with two small spawning rivers, draining into a well known salmon fishery, the Owenmore, which my copy of *Where to Fish* – the comprehensive fisherman's guide for the British Isles – did not even mention. Subsequently, in my old copy of 1984-85 it says this under the paragraph on the Owenmore River 'good for spring salmon'. So fifteen years on while fishing at the lake is mentioned there seemed to be no change to the information Charles Roberts had given me on that first visit, which was that Carrowmore was so shallow it was little more than a wet marsh over half its area.

Kenneth Cosgrove – into a fish

Then along comes the 1992 revised edition of Peter O'Reilly's *Trout and Salmon Loughs of Ireland* which states, 'this is probably the premier spring salmon fishing lough in the country at the time of writing'. Similarly on the Owenmore River 'It is every inch a brilliant salmon and sea trout fishery.' What on earth had been going on, for while the river had always been well known, nobody knows more about Irish loughs than Peter, and he is not given to purple prose unless it is fully justified! Could this really be better than Currane, or Beltra and Glencar, if so why hadn't it been promoted before?

And the answer? The local anglers took over the management of the lake, they built a small dam at the point of outflow, the water level was raised by about three feet, and before your very eyes a remarkable new fishery emerged, and what is more it has continued to improve to this day. My own record speaks for itself, for, always in poor conditions with most of the time a cold and hard wind from the north, with four days spring fishing in early May 1996, and mid-April 2000 I landed four fish, best 8½lb, including a very early grilse of 4½lb, and another springer lost with the fly snagged exactly as mentioned earlier on Loch Feagh. The flies that did the job were two taken with a Black Pennel, including the lost fish, one Green Peter, and one a Bibio and the sizes 8 to 10. One April day, with an echo sounder on the side of the boat, we could see the remarkable numbers of salmon present, often in big shoals, while the extraordinary lack of depth was also clear, hardly anywhere more than eight feet deep, with most of it between four and five! One could therefore see only too clearly why the dam was needed, being the perfect example of how sensible and constructive enhancement projects can work well, its contribution to the local economy – exactly as at Delphi and Burrishoole – of real benefit in an area where to create any form of employment is extremely difficult. While the Irish Government provided technical and financial support, it was the boys at Bangor who had the get up and go for which they are hugely to be congratulated. They saw that by giving nature a hand the scope was very real – and went on to prove it.

Driving up from the south from Newport, along the north shore of Clew Bay, Croagh Patrick high to the south over the sea, you turn north just beyond the old summer resort of Mallaranny with its Victorian houses, at the Achill turning, a narrow sea lough now on your left. Here, if you are a gardener, look out for a curious invasion of very large tree heathers that flourish both sides of the road, surely escaped from a local garden, finding the conditions of high rainfall with the wind from the ocean ideal.

One crosses first the little Ballyreeny River, just a small stream which once had a very good white trout fishing, and then the Owenduff which is a highly attractive miniature salmon/trout system which continues to have a reasonable run of spring fish. And as you get out to look over the bridge, suddenly you realise the country has completely changed – it has opened up to become 'big sky' country, so that for the first time on our journey north since Galway, while there are still mountains and hills they are no longer breathing down your neck, but are relatively a long way off. There are acres of much flatter peat-based moorland all around, with some of it worked as a commercial peat operation, and on my first visit there was a merlin, that little falcon of the open moors dashing fast away inland. While peat extraction may not be an attractive sight, the moors recover relatively quickly and as I just remarked, in such areas to create any form of employment is extremely difficult, and I also repeat that the Delphi fishery's financial contribution to that area is calculated to be £400,000 a year, something the anglers of Bangor are trying hard to match, and probably now do!

After the Owenduff bridge one turns inland to follow the line of the Owenmore, its spatey nature clearly visible in the stretch by the little town. Here the visitor can get day tickets as an alternative to the lough, and my guess is that in falling water after rain one would, at the right time of year, be odds on for a brace of fish. It is fly only fishing, by law, but this is a river made for exactly that, so that even in a flood with a sinking line and a weighted 2 inch tube I would fancy my chances.

Bangor Erris, in the best tradition, is built round a road junction and a bridge – the first one up from the sea. Coming from Newport with the route we took, turn left having crossed the bridge and it is west to Belmullet with its sheltered harbours, passing Lough Carrowmore on one's right. If you turn east you will head back inland over the moors to Crossmolina at the north end of Lough Conn, and the lush green of the limestone influence. Going that route the wide open country takes you past Bellacorick and almost the only peat-fired power station I ever saw. If you keep going after the power station and shortly take the right fork, before long you will see ahead the massive Nephin mountain, almost bare rock, and you realise you have come full circle, Lough Beltra coming up, with Newport beyond. As with the famous Ring of Kerry, Ireland has many such natural trips on offer – around Connemara for instance – and for those not fishing, this one from Newport to Bangor and back is not to be missed.

It's about time we did some fishing, so let's have a look at an article I wrote for *Trout and Salmon* magazine covering my April 2000 visit, 'Salmon on the Lake of the Ravens', with some extracts, and two days on Carrowmore.

On the first day there was hardly a breath of wind to start with and I decided to concentrate on my 11 foot single-handed Greys loch rod, with an old No 5 floater that now sinks very slowly. On the bob I had a size 8 Green Peter, dropper size 10 Black Pennel and a Claret and Blue salmon single tied on a heavy size 8 hook on the tail, with 12lb Maxima nylon. I also had a 12 foot rod with an AFTM 10 line in case a gale got up, with just two flies – a size 10 Silver Stoat double on the bob and a small treble Shrimp on the tail.

All morning the wind fooled around, settling after lunch in the north-west, maintaining a firm and steady strength, with high cloud for the rest of the day. While it was far from warm, these were perfectly possible conditions and we started to catch a few trout, which is always a good sign, as well as some very fine sea-trout smolts.

I was therefore not surprised when, in four feet of water, a fish took my Green Peter about four yards from the boat, taking some time to show us it was something a lot larger than a trout, and turning out to be a very fresh grilse of 4½lb! As it was only 17 April, this seemed to me at least a month early, but I was told another had been taken in the river a few days before – remarkable!

About fifteen minutes later, I had a more solid wrenching take of the middle dropper as another fish turned away to my right at speed, but only five seconds later the hook came out. I checked the fly and, sure enough, the wretched nylon had taken two turns round the Black Pennel's hook, giving exactly the wrong direction of pull, while the ability of the barb to become buried was gone, too. How this infuriating hang-up occurs is beyond me, but it is always the main length of leader, not the dropper arm itself, that is involved and it is very difficult to spot!

But God is indeed good, and had we not had lunch on the lake's own holy island? An hour later I had another solid take well away from the boat, which turned out to be a handsome 8lb springer. This time it was well and truly attached to the same Black Pennel. This was great fishing in far from perfect conditions and all were taken in about four feet of water.

Next day, John Cosgrove was tied up in the morning so his fifteen-year-old son Kenneth took over, with great competence. And here I must again make the point that, while the fisherman may be hooking and landing fish, it is the boatman who has found them for you. That the lies of these fish will usually be by rocks and points or river mouths and shallow banks is certainly true, but exactly which of these they prefer is impossible to guess, particularly in a lake the size of Carrowmore, which is four-and-a-half miles long and up to three miles wide and, all I can say is that Cosgroves, father and son, know all about their fishery and how to find fish.

The weather on the next day was very similar to the first, but in this case we did not get the same steady wind in the afternoon, suffering periods of flat calm. I had decided that a slow sinker might be a sensible alternative in cold conditions with the water about 43 degrees, particularly as there was little wind and a poor wave. I therefore brought into action a very good old friend a No 6, 9 foot Hardy Jet fibre-glass rod circa 1970, with a No 5 slow sinker. Attached were a size 10 shop-bought 'bumble' Bibio on the bob, one of my own nymph-like (and well-chewed) size 8 Bibios on the dropper, and a similar sized home-tied Black Pennel on the tail. With this I managed to catch a second, rather larger, grilse, which with immaculate taste chose 'my' Bibio rather than the official version – about which more later. I think I might have pulled the fly out of the mouth of another grilse, and Michael Moore, who was also fishing in the boat, had one promising looking rise without contact, while a few more trout and smolts became attached as well.

I cannot record the events of this visit without a mention of the ravens that nest on two of Carrowmore's islands, including the northern monastery site, which was our Monday lunch spot. It has a tree on it, a gnarled thorn, leaning and shaped by the prevailing wind, maximum height ten feet, and in it was a huge nest, occupied then

A 4lb grilse

by five nearly fully grown young ravens, which did as mother had told them and froze when one peered at them from a rather insecure branch. Mother, meantime, who could reasonably be expected to panic at this invasion, was taking our disturbing interest singularly calmly, observing our movements from about fifty yards (father being further off) usually from a couple of dead trees that were not far from the nest, while curiously, and very deliberately, pecking viciously at the dead wood. Was this from frustration, which it looked like, or perhaps an instinctive ruse to distract intruders, perhaps by implying that she had discovered food? All I know is that one could converse quite well by imitating their croak, and that, given that the island is used most days as a picnic spot, they expect the remains of one's lunch to be left behind, as a matter of courtesy, checking the moment we were afloat again.

Next day, on another island at the southern end of the lake, there was another pair of ravens to talk to with an even larger nest, and the hen bird went through exactly the same pecking routine as had its cousin the day before. Conrad Laurenz, the great ornithologist and anthropologist (who wrote *King Solomon's Ring* and *Man*

Lough Carrowmore – the outflow

Meets Dog) thought ravens were, after man, the most intelligent creatures on this earth since they could reason. As an example, he quoted the occasion when, out for a walk, his tame raven who was with him came in great distress to tell him his dog had fallen through the ice of the frozen Danube, and that his help was urgently needed. Similarly, Aylmer Tryon in *The Quiet Waters By* reports on the antics of ravens in Iceland which 'attach themselves to the farms in winter', and 'are regarded as pets, sometimes teasing the sheepdogs!' I asked him about this and he confirmed it was entirely deliberate, the birds having fun pulling the dogs' tails! On Carrowmore the approach is less subtle but real for all that, for if these strange fishermen want to bring us lunch, why should we be scared of them, anyway? I found them fascinating, these huge glossy black birds of great power, nearly half as big again as a crow or rook, as does Kenneth, and I hope he continues to make them his friends.

But back to the fishing and one rather startling question does arise from my two days catching three fish, which should have been four. I am too old to worry about accusations of conceit, but the fact is that despite five or six boats fishing, say ten rods involved, nobody else caught a thing, which does call for a long, hard look at what I was doing which they were not! To start with, since the actual flies that caught the fish are very different from typical versions on offer, there are some facts for consideration.

While I can and do tie the big bumble patterns much promoted by Kingsmill Moore, almost the only version I ever use is the Zulu in heavy dark conditions, when for big sea trout in particular it is deadly, and a very basic Claret Bumble, which catches a lot of brown trout, too. Clearly, these bear little resemblance to the real thing, and my ideas of a Black Pennel or Bibio are similarly eccentric. As I recorded above I was in fact given a Bibio by Charles Roberts, its inventor at Burrishoole in 1969, being far closer to my version than is today's usual bumble. Similarly it was Tony O'Sullivan at Waterville who insisted the traditional Black Pennels we had brought with us on our first visit in 1970 were no good, heavy seal's fur bodies with broad silver bands being vital, an opinion he, and we as followers, were to prove correct time after time.

Carrowmore – a good easy wave

But obviously it is not just the flies that count, the way they are moved in the water being equally critical, not least because, since salmon do not feed in freshwater, each and every take must therefore be an 'induced' take. It matters not what it is that induces this reaction, it is a hunter's reaction to what might be an escaping food source. The point is to attract the fish's attention and then to move the lure in a manner that experience shows prompts a reaction to grab it, for which there are a variety of methods available.

As the boat drifted down wind I was casting a long line, covering 45 degrees ahead of my position. In all cases the fish took during a quite fast retrieve, created by the longest possible sweep of my free arm – about 5 feet. Similarly, which is important, the rod point started low, being progressively raised, with its upward movement restricted to the brief pause when the line was not being recovered by hand! By this means a constant, and quite quick, rate of recovering is achieved by the flies, which on balance for both salmon and sea trout appears to do the trick most of the time.

Carrowmore from the north

But one must be flexible in one's technique as this is certainly not always the case, for sometimes a very short line with a big bumble or Green Peter sedge pattern on the bob is all they will look at. And note, my first grilse that took the Green Peter, did so quite close to the boat when the fly was just starting to cut the surface. So, in the end, it boils down to trial and error. Whatever the method used, aim for perfection with every cast, and that calls for a balanced outfit, continuous concentration and practice – and in my case I have been practising fishing from boats for fifty-five years!

On last year's trip I was at Bangor on 15 and 16 August, having a day on Carrowmore with Kenneth, father John Cosgrove again tied up, being very different from the cold spring days there before. A minor spate just before I arrived had removed the sea trout up into their spawning streams, those left in the lough were the typically small 'juniors' that average under 1lb in weight. Their presence, however, generated activity, while the odd salmon put its nose up, Kenneth making contact with a grilse, while I rose and never touched one or two others. It was far from good fishing weather, a hard breeze from the north-west, with typical broken clouds producing a glaring light. These were for Sidney Spencer, a west coast lough fisherman all his life, his most disliked conditions, and mine too!

But Kenneth showed what could be done with a grilse – and well done!

The syndicate also has fishing on the Owenmore River that I have only looked at but I liked what I saw. This must be a superb bonus to have on your doorstep as a local resident, for this river has been considered one of Ireland's finest spate rivers since the 1800s – fly only by law, going back to those days! It opens on 1 February with a spring run, 20lb fish not uncommon, with then the grilse, followed by some big autumn salmon as well.

There are no hotels in Bangor, but comprehensive 'B&B' facilities which may produce evening meals, for which my friend Evelyn Cosgrove at Hillcrest is a perfect example. However not that far away at the village of Geesala, a new hotel is now open – the Teach Iorrgis Hotel – for those wanting different surroundings.

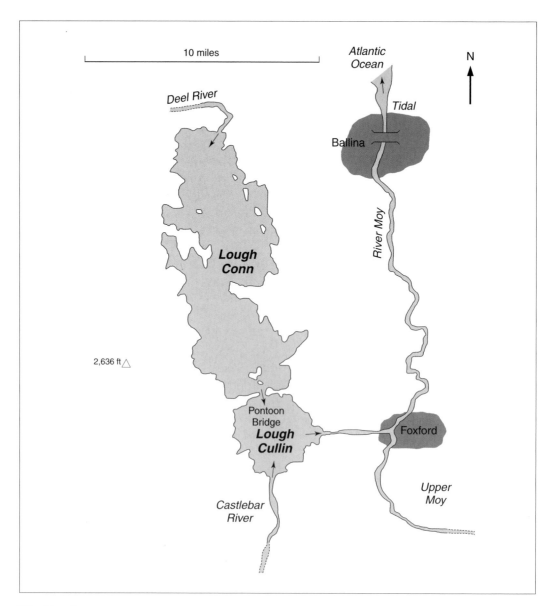

The Moy System

Chapter 17

The Moy System

As with the Corrib, I had not planned to include in this book the River Moy, despite its associated Loughs Conn and Cullin, because the book is primarily about salmon and sea trout lough fishing, and not rivers, while again these famously are great brown trout lakes. However, exactly as with the Galway river fishery and Corrib, my friends told me I was wrong, and that anyone going to fish in the west of Ireland may sensibly have in mind a visit to such a great fishery as a possible option, and anyway the loughs produce a lot of salmon too! I stand corrected! The river seems to average about 8000 salmon a year, taken largely between Ballina at the top of the tide, and Foxford, with not much more than ten miles involved. This is a massive return per mile by any standards, while the estimate I was once given for the lakes was over five hundred salmon on Conn and two hundred from Cullin, although as with Corrib there are hardly any sea trout. This absence illustrates vividly that it is above all the shortage of food which makes sea trout migrate, or starve – it is 'force majeure' – stay and remain small or go to sea and grow fat!

Here are perhaps the finest wild salmon rearing waters anywhere, the limestone base providing a huge volume of food, with an excellent range of spawning rivers available. It therefore is hard to imagine what sort of fishery improvement programme could be needed but they have just that and one costing around £2 million. And, incredibly, the system does have scope for very considerable uplift, because the large majority of salmon running the river turn right just above Foxford into the Cross River that drains Loughs Cullin and Conn, in that order, so that the run ignores very largely the Moy itself as it swings east. This has considerable potential as a spawning area, and the decision to develop its productive possibilities will make a fascinating story to follow.

The riparian ownership of the river is to some extent fragmented so that a united owners' front does not seem to be much in evidence. However with the North West Fisheries Board extremely active, river management is clearly first class, while the proof of success is there for all to see, and thousands come to catch salmon – many who never had dreamed they would ever get to grips with the king of fish!

Against its appearance twenty-five years ago, when I had a day on the lower river, a lot of changes have taken place. In fact my first look at the river had been during our original trip to Newport when we decided a day after salmon would be an idea, not realising the horrific damage the vast arterial drainage scheme had caused: a sunk river, slow and canal like and the banks piles of sand and gravel with almost nowhere I could see where a fly could fish as it should. We spent an hour or so chucking spinners about and went home! Today with the banks grassed over and trees well grown in places, the moonscape is much improved, while in places the flow of the river seems somewhat better. But it is a long way from most salmon rivers, and very definitely a bait fisher's water.

In March 1975 I had the famous Ridge Pool to myself for a day with an old boatman – needed as in fact one fished from a sort of punt when the tide was in. I was surprised by the boat that was uncomfortable and difficult to fish from but I felt one had a chance with every cast that I made. And a friend had, not that long before, taken in one day twenty-two salmon, only half being grilse, from exactly where I was then fishing but it had been in May. As it was a cold day and his 'man' had said only a spinner would catch a fish, he began with a spoon in high water below the traps, getting fish with his second and sixth casts. He promptly changed over to his fly rod with which he landed another twenty salmon in six hours! Some fishing and still quite possible today.

In those days a large percentage of salmon running the Moy finished up in the traps immediately above the Ridge Pool which subsequently were removed. That day in March I saw in the few hours I was fishing half a dozen good spring fish extracted just above me, and I asked the man on duty, after I had stopped fishing, about the numbers that the traps took. He answered 'by the ton – but it leaves plenty – and I'm a keen fisherman too!'

It may be that the Moy then had a big spring run of fish, but I doubt it does now and that will in no way imply bad management by those into whose hands that task has been thrust today. In fact very possibly the ability of the Moy system, unaided, to produce such a vast number of returning adult salmon and grilse should become a major and detailed scientific study, not least because it is a huge, low cost, food producer! With such rearing facilities, is it really not possible to follow the Icelandic pattern of commercial salmon production by ranching on a massive scale, and thereby getting rid of the cages and their associated parasites?

As we now know, because of the concentrations of fish that cage farms involve, they provide the ideal environment for sea lice. In entirely natural conditions lice are faced as juveniles with a survival outlook that is massively odds against! For they are host specific, being only able to survive in almost all cases on the species 'salar', which in the case of salmon but not sea trout do no more than pass through their estuarine habitat, giving them little opportunity to attach themselves to their specific 'hosts', essential for their survival. Both returning adults and migrating smolts provide them with suitable facilities, with for the latter extremely small lice, invisible to the eye, infesting their immature bodies where they grow fast, often covering a small sea trout smolt from head to tail, making it black and unrecognisable.

And as we all now know, while salmon smolts push on out into the ocean making their exposure to lice more limited, sea trout that hang around estuaries are far more vulnerable, with whole populations almost destroyed as we saw at Delphi and in

The Moy – the old traps

Connemara. But as I also saw at Delphi, Costello and Ballynahinch recently it could just be that a critical turning point has been reached. Meanwhile on the Moy system, highly successfully sea trout fishing does take place in the estuary, but not in the loughs or the river Moy itself, with spawning presumably in other smaller streams up and down the coast.

The fact that Lough Conn attracts international competitions underlines its excellence as a trout fishery, while a lot of salmon are caught on the fly as a by product, something for which the wise angler is prepared. The same flies – sizes 8 to 12 – will do the job, for despite their far greater bulk lake salmon in my experience prefer smaller sizes than do both sea and brown trout most of the time. But be sure to have a good big net, and unless conditions are so bright that one must go lighter, your nylon should not be less than 7lb, and up to 10lb in a big wave and heavy cloud or rain. If with your 10 foot rod you hook a 10lb fish, you must make him fight so keep up the pressure, rod point always high to give maximum spring, but ease off instantly if he jumps.

As with all major loughs there is no substitute for having a boatman at least for your early visits, and on beyond if you can afford it. While areas of a lake favoured by brown trout, with food the main factor, tend not to change, with salmon this is by no means the case, so that a particular stretch of shore, at one time much favoured, can be abandoned for no visible reason. That said well established lies continue to draw fish year after year, in this case, taking Cullin first, at the railway bridge in the lake around the outflow, through which many thousands of salmon and grilse must pass, and the narrows at Pontoon Bridge, being the inflow from Conn. And in that lough, which with 14,000 acres is not short of space, while you can also fish around the narrows and the immediate islands, the general advice for salmon is to head for the northern end, into which flows the main spawning river, the Deel.

I had a day on this river a few years ago, more out of curiosity than anything else, for surely a very considerable run of salmon must enter its waters. What is more, given some will be springers that tend to head for the upper streams quickly, there should be good fishing in May with the right conditions. That I was there in July, after little rain for some weeks, meant that I can't say I fished with much hope, but low down towards the lough near Deel Castle I could see considerable scope, while upstream looking over bridges I felt that, possibly because the Moy itself is so good and close by, this could easily be another forgotten fishery, not unlike the Clare at Corrib.

At the southern extreme of the loughs the Manulla River enters Lough Cullin and provides good spring salmon fishing, Peter O'Reilly referring to some two hundred taken each year. But on where to try for salmon on your own, in either lough the presence of a feeder stream is always worth investigation, for often very late in the season remarkably small flows of water become surprisingly larger, so that salmon, their backs out of the water, will make a quick dash from the lake to spawn.

To improve safety, much has been done in the lakes to reduce the risk of hitting rocks by marking them with iron bars, something that newcomers in particular will welcome.

While all of this sounds as though the Moy system's salmon fishing is almost perfect, the drainage for me has ruined the river and only limited fly water is available, while thanks to the remarkable numbers of fish present its popularity makes shoulder to shoulder here again a fact. This, however, is entirely a matter of personal taste and what one can afford to pay for one's sport. But for me, less good fishing in wild country away from it all rates much higher than a crowded beat full of fish in a built up area – except to see what it's like. And in this case there is no doubt that, since the government bought out the Moy Fishery Company twenty years ago, they have been responsible for excellent management, with in 1989 the total declared catch being 11,075 salmon and grilse.

There is a delightful country house on the west bank of Lough Conn, Enniscoe House, which reminds me very much of Carrarevagh House on Corrib. If there is a better place for a house party for the mayfly it would be difficult to imagine it. Here also Barry Seagrave runs a fishery advice service, having a wide range of connections up and down the west coast, including detailed knowledge of where is fishing well and where is not – very handy for the casual, or infrequent visiting angler.

Chapter 18

The North-West

Suddenly I was getting a bit out of my depth, for although I had looked at the region before as I drove through it, I had only twice fished in the west north of the Moy River – very briefly twenty years ago in the Rosses area on a trip to gather detail for some fishing articles. This had also involved fishing Lough Eske, in Donegal, a salmon lough not to be ignored, albeit the two grilse I rose decided not to take hold of my Black Pennel properly. Perhaps I should have been using a Donegal Blue, as a matter of courtesy, but in the gentle wind of that day, while nothing held on, I could see the fishery's considerable and obvious potential. Here it was that Hugh Falkus and Sidney Spencer fished together, their boatman my own guide when I was there. In general terms Falkus preferred rivers to lakes, while Spencer liked the reverse, although neither disliked the alternative. For myself I refuse to think in terms of one or the other for there is so much to draw one to so many entirely different venues.

Think of mayfly on a great chalk stream – or Lough Sheelin – the Spey at Ballindallach in May as a heavy winter's snow melts up in the tops – a quiet June night on the Towy with the big sea trout awake – Currane in early July full of fish – the Tay in September with hosts of salmon up to 40lb, and even better on a frozen March day at Stanley with springers averaging at least 15lb, straight from the sea – and a picture almost replicated at Careysville on the Cork Blackwater.

In my view one cannot run a beauty competition with fisheries as so many have utterly differing attractions, for instance the unique little Wye in Derbyshire where rainbows live and breed, unlike any other river in these islands. And in much the same way the truly complete angler will always remain flexible, being able to learn new techniques (in Montana with a dry fly I learned the upstream mend in the air, while casting) right up to the day you hang up your rod, and net, and boots, for the last time.

Meanwhile bear this thought in mind, a proposition given me by an old Yorkshire fly fisherman, with a double first in classics at Baliol, that a good day's wild trout fishing was always achieved if the angler came home with 5lb of fish in his creel! Think about that: one of 5lb, twenty of a quarter, or two of 2 ½lb! Not far wrong in my view!

All my fishing life I had read about, and seen reported the fishing activities of Lough Melvin and its four mile river, linking it to the sea, the River Drowse the earliest river in Europe, opening day 1 January, with in most years a salmon taken. This fishery is as the departing ice left it eleven thousand years ago, and no less a person than

Charles McLaren told me once he thought the system had to be absolutely unique, and he was not given to exaggeration, or indeed selling Scotland's loch fisheries short. Similarly another great fisherman and riparian manager, Frank Sawyer of Netheravon, fished Melvin once and reported much the same reaction.

With these fisheries are also just to the south, the very considerable loughs Gill and another Glencar, which we will look at next. Meanwhile with curious flat-top mountains, and the Atlantic wind ever with you, the fisherman's sensitive feelers will stir as he comes this way – rightly for this is a productive area.

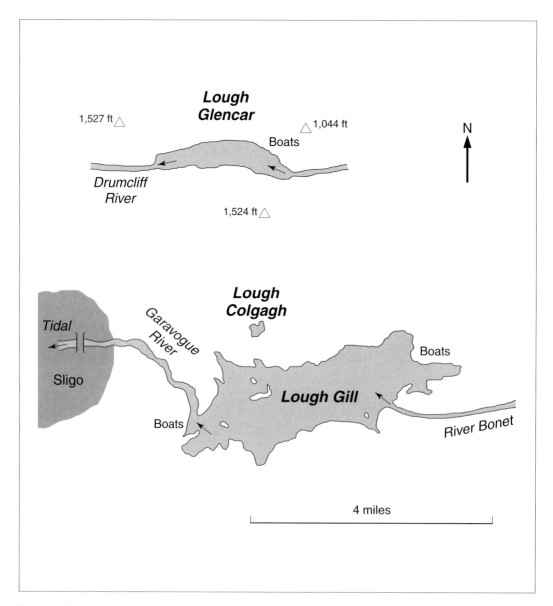

Loughs Gill and Glencar

Chapter 19

Loughs Gill and Glencar

As we head on north towards considerable hills and mountains, it is not far from the Moy to Lough Gill and the River Garavogue at Sligo, our route crossing, a few miles short of the town, the Ballysodare River. This is an unusual river in that it took an Act of Parliament in 1837 to get the system's salmon fishing rights into the hands of the Cooper family of Markree Castle, as a 'quid pro quo' for building substantial fish passes round the Ballysodare Falls, which until then blocked the river one hundred per cent. The Ballysodare River itself is only five miles long but it drains 252 square miles of area through its two major tributaries, the Owenmore draining Templehouse Lake, and the Unshin that carries the outflow from Lough Arrow no less, making it an important all round river system. However, as with other systems where the food supply is so good, sea trout are in very short supply. There is a prolonged hatch of mayfly throughout the system and this is yet another highly prolific river, the catch of salmon below the falls, I was told, getting on for 1000 in a good year – mostly being grilse.

Lough Gill

The Lough Gill system, draining a variety of flat-topped hill ranges, consists of first the short Garavogue River, just three-and-a-half miles from the sea up through Sligo, then six-and-a-half miles of lake and then nearly thirty miles of the River Bonet which drains the waters of Glendale Lough high in the headwaters. It is a long way from being a typical western Irish fishery, its prime feature the spring salmon run, and the fact that grilse do not for once dominate the picture as has become so common elsewhere. In fact the whole pattern is much more like an east coast river than a western fishery, with here again remarkably few sea trout either.

Nor is the lake itself typical of the majority of Irish loughs, being somehow out of a Japanese print, thanks perhaps to the mountains being close by, with in some parts cliffs of solid rock rising directly out of the water. But its most curious feature in terms of fishing concerns the fact that, bar the mayfly season when the brown trout fishing is good, it is almost exclusively a spring salmon fishery which ends at the end of May, although with grilse taken from the Bonet upstream some should be caught in the lake on their way there. Almost all the salmon fishing on Gill is done by trolling, and the season starts on the 1 January with February and March said to be the best time to be there, and come June salmon fishing has ended, the take these days three hundred or so of solid spring fish.

While I was over recently I spent some time looking at the Bonet at both summer levels and in flood, which was a formidable sight given that much of its course descends quite fast. This is a very considerable spate river with I should guess real potential for development as a seriously good salmon river, another to join the underrated ranks of the Deel and Clare, each having the characteristic that they feed loughs from above, with the ocean on beyond. While with the two latter rivers first-class fisheries exist below their associated loughs – the Moy and Galway – in this case the Garavogue only produces a handful of springers which seems curious, as they must pass through in considerable numbers, although the grilse fishing is of greater interest, and some sea trout are taken.

Above the lake the Bonet produces spring fish from March onwards, right up to Manorhamilton where the local angling club has seven miles of water with grilse from July onwards, and plenty of September fish to be had in good water. Lower down Dromhair Lodge has several miles of river that I had planned to fish, only to be washed out by a big spate, being due to head south the next day. Further on down, just above the lake the river continued to look good, a variety of possible fisheries available to the visitor.

I have no doubt, after some serious local research, that the Bonet could offer excellent spring salmon fishing in April given reasonable conditions of water and weather. On this strong flowing river you would do far better with a solid double-handed fly rod to cover the water and handle heavy fish, than with a single-hander. This is another fishery I want to go back to.

Lastly on this subject, while Lough Glendale at the top of the river looks every inch the part of salmon lake, I was told that although some fish got through the results were only modest. What a pity as the setting in the mountains is glorious.

Gill is fed by the excellent Bonet River – in spate

Just a mile or so north of Lough Gill, down below the Sligo to Manorhamilton road is a little lough that to a fisherman who stops up on the hill where the road is, absolutely breathes fish! This is Colgagh Lough, under a hundred acres, a couple of boats pulled up on the shore, home of substantial brownies, average 1½lb with 5lb fish often netted. My limited enquiries locally produced little reaction but Peter O'Reilly did better and his book is as enthusiastic as I am. Here on a quiet summer evening with the right ripple, a big sedge could work wonders for the big ones almost into the dark. If you get that chance grab it with both hands!

Also, but further north of Gill is Lough Glencar, in a spectacular valley between the King Mountains to the north and Crockauns to the south, with miles of geological strata visible high on the hillsides, and its own remarkable waterfall at the eastern end a popular tourist attraction.

Glencar Lough – the north shore

Glencar looking west

The Drumcliff River drains the lake just four miles to the sea, which looked at in low water did not seem to offer much in terms of fishing. However there is a run of spring salmon and grilse, a number taken from the various pools present, plus an excellent stock of sea trout, which enjoy an above average weight. These of course will end up in the lough, where chatting to some fishermen about to launch their boat, I was told that by then, mid-August, you would be very surprised to get a salmon, a few grilse about, but that the sea trout were doing well, with one of the anglers enthusiastic about use of the dapp! They also said that in the mayfly season one could catch sea trout with a dry fly, keeping it moving all the time, as one once could on Beltra.

The lough is deep to the south and much shallower along the north shore, shelving as it goes south. This means that good areas of fishable water are available for the fly fisherman, the only method allowed from boats, and what a terrific change from all that trolling! While perhaps not Currane or Carrowmore I am certain that this fishery has very real potential.

Gill – a quiet corner

As I mentioned above, the Unshin River drains Lough Arrow which is one of Ireland's greatest brown trout loughs. With an ability, thanks to that limestone again, to produce wild trout of a size that almost equal salmon, and four weeks of mayfly from mid-May to mid-June, combined with a variety of duckfly, olives, buzzers and sedges, this is a superb fishery from March to September. In fact so good that a Lough Sheelin resident I met there when on a 'spent gnat' trip, admitted he thought that Arrow had overtaken his own Sheelin. To which he added, do not ignore Lough Key, just east of Arrow, when the mayfly were going well.

The quality of the fishing that is on offer in western Ireland is truly remarkable, with 5lb or 6lb wild brown trout available to back up their salmon and sea trout, often costing almost nothing, or indeed entirely free. Long may it last.

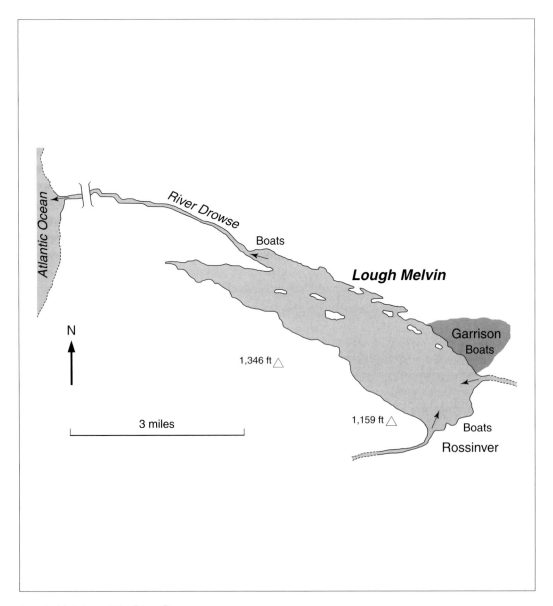

Lough Melvin and the River Drowse

Chapter 20

Lough Melvin and the River Drowse

We have reached our northern limit, it is sheeting with rain, and I have just filled my car with petrol in Eire, at a cost which is about one third less than it would have been at Garrison, just over the border in Ulster. I was at Rossinver for a meeting with one of the major contributors to the Irish fishing world, Terence Bradley, guardian and champion of this great lough for many years, and now, at a remarkable age you would never guess, retired to his house on Rossinver Bay a stone's throw from that lake's shore.

Lough Melvin at Garrison

And Lough Melvin must truly be one of nature's best maintained and least damaged lakes, hardly it seems changed since the ice left it, mountains to the south, and ocean to the west via the River Drowse, the total catchment not great at 103 square miles. It therefore is not a big system with the lough about eight miles long and nearly two miles wide at the eastern end, where the two quite small spawning rivers enter. There are several good sized and fertile looking islands, with mainly on the north shore a number of points and bays, all contributing towards a picture that shouts at the angler to get fishing! Which impression is fully borne out by results that record consistently not only high numbers of fish taken by fishermen, but for one lake an almost unique variety of game fish well represented. While many loughs may have a lot of brown trout and salmon, with say a token number of char, Melvin has its different species all in serious numbers.

Looking at this variety in detail, salmon come from the sea early and the 1 January opening date on the Drowse regularly provides the first British Isles salmon of the year, while Melvin has to wait a month for their season to open on 1 February. Grilse arrive in June, running fast up to the lake, but for reasons we have already discussed here again there are no sea trout, the only major game fish missing.

There are four types of trout, scientifically similar but clearly each a sub-species that is obvious to the eye. They include ferox, gillaroo, and sonaghan with of course brown trout which are present in huge numbers, a 1985 competition recording 759 trout to 114 anglers in a single day – exactly how many of which sub-species not recorded. The ferox grow fat on small perch and the char which are also present, and the gillaroo specialise in the consumption of shrimps, snails and molluscs as a whole, for which they have developed a second gizzard, which is reflected in the depth of their body. On which score, above Loch Assynt in Sutherland is a small limestone loch named Gillaroo, where gillaroo trout were and perhaps still are to be found, although now somewhat rarely I hear, but I did catch two in a day there in the middle 1970s, their identity confirmed both by Willie Morrison, the hotel and fishery owner, and by dissection. There is no record of the loch being stocked with gillaroos, and in the Inchnadamph Hotel in a Victorian glass case are a pair of fine fish of about 3 to 4lb! How did they get there, or can nature adapt so easily?

Melvin was where Kingsmill Moore started his serious career as a fisherman, a school friend's family owning a large house on its shore, the father – unlike the judge's who didn't fish at all – his much respected, and strict, tutor. He interestingly says this about the fourth species I mentioned:

The sonaghan, which is not, as far as I know, found elsewhere, provides most of the sport . . . it is rarely over a pound and a half in weight; lives in deeper water than other trout . . . and seems to move in small shoals. Free rising, very strong for its weight, . . . it can give a sparkling day . . . A complete contrast to the gillaroo which haunts rocky shores!

What a place in which to learn!

Lough Melvin from the south

Melvin has both shallows and deep areas which of course suit the char and the ferox who prey on them, which depths, it now turns out, are also a haven for large spring salmon too. And this intelligence – confirmed at Delphi with the deeps of Doo Lough involved – was entirely new to me, being a complete contradiction of the traditional view that salmon always stay close to the surface, very often almost touching adjacent rocks or points, hugging as well underwater ridges and banks. But with modern technology it seems that to spot a salmon sixty feet down in a lake is basic stuff, levels at which the professional char fishermen of Windermere used to take their toll in years past.

For salmon the eastern end of the lake is best for the early fish, the Garrison area being trolled hard from opening day, and some say too hard at that, with four rods per boat in action. While I doubt fish are foul hooked, this does seem to me well over the top, questioning whether it can be described as sport at all but then they may be fishing either for the pot or to sell what they catch or both. South of the border in

Ireland this is now illegal, the tagging system introduced to make sure the law can be enforced! How soon before Ulster, and why not the whole United Kingdom, follows suit?

If you enjoy it you can also troll for ferox which, pound for pound, have strength that in my view cannot be beaten, even by the wild rainbows of the Rockies. But for me Melvin has got to be a fly fisherman's paradise, for in Rossinver Bay the salmon take the fly well and here, with my 12 foot light split cane McLaren two-hander, which Charles McLaren himself showed us once how to use on the television in a programme filmed on Lough Melvin, I would expect to do well. Today they told me that the salmon catch was a third to the fly – against Garrison say ten per cent which as we have seen is by today's standards high. But if Carrowmore's catch is all on fly, post 1 April with no trolling – only spinning from the boat allowed before that which I find just as boring as trailing baits behind a boat – what might not be achieved on Melvin too. Meanwhile at Currane today the ratio must be fifty per cent fly for salmon, with so many taken while after sea trout, more and more anglers wanting to

The Drowse River meets the sea

Middle Drowse – lovely fly water

succeed in a manner whereby the angler's participation is so much greater, a view upon which increasing numbers of European visitors in particular appear to concur. It's not easy to get a lake salmon to take your fly, but it is quite possible, and every one on a fly – your own homemade the best, being fished with real skill as it must be – is worth ten on the troll. I beg anyone starting now to fish lakes with salmon in them to work at it, succeed and you will never look back.

Perhaps today one should call the Drowse River 'The People's River' for that was precisely what was intended by its owner Thomas Gallagher when he bought it. The daily charge remains £10, there are almost no reservable beats, numbers of fishermen are unlimited for its four-and-a-half miles, and all legal means of fishing are allowed. The only places where some reservation is to be seen is at the top, just below the lough, where some superb fly water is available that the adjacent holiday bungalows owned by the fishery can take. I talked to several visiting anglers during

Drowse – just up from the tide.

my last visit, just before we had a considerable storm of rain. All had the highest praise for the fishery, one old man having fished the river many years ago and was re-visiting, who said he thought if anything it appeared that more fish were now being caught than had been the case in the 1950s.

As I have made no bones about it several times in our journey up the west coast, I very much value the remote element that mostly comes with salmon and sea trout fishing, something I fear would be hard to find in really good fishing conditions on the Drowse. A river is a Venturi that, like it or not, must condense salmon shoals that linger in its waters making them highly vulnerable. And it is a curious fact that with very small rivers, which have lakes up river as potential safe havens, fish entering from the sea on a spate will run flat out inland to that lake. So, you see, it's bred into them, and it's instinctive, which clearly it should be. However they all do not behave that way, and a number of salmon will be found in rivers below such lakes, including extremely red fish late in the year, being there to spawn, offspring of parents who also spawned below the lough, and the Drowse late on has its share of exactly such

Melvin – not a fishing day!

red fish. That they have been up to Melvin as early springers, and subsequently dropped back, may be the case, something that with smaller rivers is common. In any event they should be returned, as the idea that a truly red salmon will smoke perfectly well is nonsense – by far the best smoked salmon comes from absolutely fresh fish, straight out of the tide!

Thomas Gallagher was extremely interesting to talk to, as were the team at Rossinver. This system takes itself and its fishing facilities truly seriously, and has every intention of maintaining the highest possible standards. That these may not be quite those that existed when the judge was a boy seems certain although the salmon targets of around 1000 for the Drowse and 300 or so at Rossinver seem to be maintained. The trawling efforts by the fishmongers of Garrison were the only sour note that I detected, and while the shoulder to shoulder efforts low down on the river were not to my personal taste, with the minimal costs involved, it gives everyone a chance to catch a salmon!

Here you could, in your retirement, fish the whole season through, and on the lough do well with the Kingsmill, the judge's fly first developed for Melvin. Unique is not too strong a word for this fishery. Just how, or why, it seems to be able to maintain its remarkable standards and retain its fish numbers is difficult to understand – but it most certainly does. This is a holiday coastline with lots of hotels, 'B&Bs' and cottages to rent, so visiting anglers have plenty of choice, whth non-fishing members of the family area also well served.

Since my meeting with him for the first time in 2001, that great contributor to Ireland's fishing, Thomas Gallagher has died. He was a very special person. His belief that to be able to catch a salmon at a price most people could afford made him generous beyond belief in his pricing policy. His huge enthusiasm and energy will long be remembered and very much missed.

Chapter 21

Lough Fishing – General Considerations

This is not a text book, nor is it intended to be a teaching manual. However, to the extent that it sets out to help fishermen who may be new to lough fishing for salmon and sea trout in Ireland, it is a guide with which some comment on the angling techniques employed, plus the equipment needed, seems appropriate. By trial and error over many years, and not least by watching with great care how others achieve success, my own strike rate has grown progressively, and I hope therefore that my observations on methods may help others, while in no way being taken as dogma!

I have written over the years a good many articles on fly fishing from boats, something I have been doing since my first trip to Scotland's north-west in 1946. With the war over, at the Inchnadamph hotel in western Sutherland we had a family 'all together again' holiday, it being an old haunt of my father's from the 1920s, having numerous hill lochs, as well as mighty Loch Assynt on our doorstep, with the result that I became an immediate enthusiast. I could fish a bit already, improbably learning the rudiments in Japan when my father was in Tokyo as our naval attaché, and then during the war in Cornwall, on the Camel and Fowey. I also love, to this day, messing about in boats, and enjoy hugely an expedition out from Padstow or Fowey trailing spinners or feathering for mackerel, or even from Loe for sharks. I therefore was very much at home in a boat chasing trout.

Casting a fly onto moving water that carries it down to a known lie, or likely spot in a river, calls for minimal action by the fisherman, but on a lake the reverse is the case, where the fly(s) is moved by oneself, and the initiative is in the angler's hands – which I like. What is more, while fish are often quite visible in rivers making them deliberate targets, in loughs they are mainly invisible, albeit both white trout, and more so salmon, will leap out of the water. Indeed salmon in lakes will sometimes, for no obvious reason, suddenly start jumping all over the place, showing one conveniently where to find them, being usually exactly where your boatman has been telling you that they are anyway. But most of the time, particularly when on a major lough that is some miles long, you are faced with a huge blank area of water, sometimes flat calm, often remarkably rough, and the fish could be anywhere.

Therefore the first task is to place yourself in your boat, somewhere where the fish are present in fair numbers, and then induce one from this imagined and invisible host, to take a fly that, in most cases, bears almost no resemblance whatsoever to any insect that is visible. And in fact, bar the odd daddy longlegs blown over the water from the lakeside or perhaps a fall of ant, a regular event in the west, almost no insects seem to be present anyway – other than midges! However, even if the place was alive with an immediate supply of Alders or March Browns which are normal food for most fish, because salmon do not feed in fresh water (and while small 'grilse' sea trout do their large and mature cousins hardly bother) your quarry becomes an even more improbable taker of a fly as something that is nourishing.

Of course this whole subject has been debated endlessly over the years, often in my view attributing sophisticated motives to fish that can be highly imaginative. One of the more logical being that the protective instinct exhibited by the cock fish towards his mate leads to the driving away of large flies, or particularly big spinning lures, certainly making sense in rivers, where paired fish will lie together prior to spawning, but not something which they do in lakes. Similarly the idea that a salmon will attack a lure out of irritation, caused by invasion of its comfortable and selected residence, is understandable in the tight confines of a river. There a large prawn fly often gets results when repeatedly 'bounced' off a salmon's nose, but again this concept makes little sense in the vastness of a typical salmon lough – except perhaps at points of inflow, which are almost a river anyway!

But to go back to basics, there are, I believe, a few simple factors that dominate the whole subject which are:

- a salmon is a hunter that catches its food in order to live
- the food concerned – from the fry stage onwards – consists entirely of other creatures, many of which will try to escape to avoid capture
- the only means available for a salmon to get hold of something is by grabbing it with its mouth
- in exactly the same way that a well fed cat will grab at a feather on a string pulled past its nose, the salmon's reaction, to a potential food source escaping, instinctively may be to prevent it from doing so
- the fish needs to be awake and alert for it to react
- maximum alertness is governed by water temperature, and oxygen content, and the state of the lough or river – i.e. is it rising or falling, is the lake rough or calm etc.

The syndrome therefore is largely that which led to the ancient saying 'it was curiosity that killed the cat', so therefore if we want to catch salmon then the same principles apply. And this is particularly the case in loughs where fish have to be drawn to a lure, often from some distance away, which you sometimes will see clearly in a big wave as a salmon, or large trout, comes after your fly. Nor should the idea get around that when trailing a bait behind a boat you are searching the depths as in a deep river pool you will get down with a heavy spinner or metal tube fly. Trailed spinners seldom go more than three feet below the surface, and a fly only half that.

Therefore I can say that I believe that for salmon, and to a lesser extent sea trout over 5lb weight, the whole art of lough fishing relates to an ability to stimulate in fish curiosity, combined with the belief that something that could be beneficial to them is about to escape and that to check out the position they must catch that something escaping with their mouth.

To most of which you may well say so what? If I am doing the right thing and catching fish, why do I have to know why, or how the method works? For which the answer is that a variety of techniques are involved to reflect a variety of differing circumstances, albeit often only quite minor differences in the way that you work your flies are required to stimulate that curiosity and response. We will look at this in the next chapter.

Many people believe that lough fishing is largely a matter of 'chuck and chance it'. Nothing could be further from the truth, as the results achieved by those who know what they are doing demonstrate time after time. Stay at any fishing hotel, on the waters I have described, where between six and ten boats are fishing each day, and you will find the same people most of the time return with the largest baskets of fish. While many will have decades of experience, producing results almost by instinct, other more inquisitive anglers, particularly those teaching their children to fish, will have spent some time thinking about how and why things happen.

Nearly always the most successful boat fishermen will cast a neat and accurate line, with minimum fuss, with seldom any false casting. This involves skill since, when lifted from the water after the flies have been retrieved, there is little line to play with on the back cast, and therefore little weight against which to bend the rod to activate the spring that projects the line forward. Very quick double hauling – precisely timed – is a help, while if the line is thrown forward high ahead of you, this will obtain maximum wind support, which can be a real contributor to distance.

In this there is no substitute for practice and, even after so many years experience I find it takes at least one day to get back to where I left off, very often the previous season. It is a help to have a bit of a warm-up at home on a lawn, or in the local park, before you set forth, but the blustery real life conditions of a boat on a lough are very different.

Before we look at the actual styles of fishing that can be employed on a lough, a check on the equipment most of us old hands would take with us for a fortnight's trip to Ireland's west coast, shows something of the variety of possibilities open to anglers.

Friends and family have often asked, as I unpack my car on arrival at the start of a lough fishing holiday, why I have so may rods, and 'surely two or three would do'. We will come to how to use them in detail later, but first one must know in general terms what I need them for, since each bit of equipment has a particular task. In my case I will have rods for both river and lough fishing, not all being dual purpose.

Salmon Fly
Double Handed–   15ft river No 10
            –   12ft river and lough No 8
            –   12ft lough No 5

Lough Fly
Single Handed – 11ft No 5
                 – 10ft No 4

Dual Purpose Fly
Single Handed – 9ft No 9
                 – 9ft No 7
                 – 9ft No 5

Spinnning and Trolling
                 – 10ft medium
                 – 9ft heavy

You will note the absence of a dapping rod, a method that I seem to be able to do without given my very light 12 foot specialist loch rod, 'The McLaren' sold to me by Charles McLaren himself! It is a three-piece cane rod designed to cope with the extremely light line essential when working the bob fly slowly in the surface. By this means the effect is almost the same as with dapping, and for me much more interesting fishing. It is not a rod for a really big wind, when one needs a heavier line which my other 12 foot rod handles perfectly – a quite old Farlow fibreglass creation, designed by John Ashley-Cooper, and like him a great killer of fish – as some rods seem to be.

It is also perfectly possible to fish my Bruce and Walker 15 foot rod from a boat, using a light line to excellent effect, but you do want to be fishing very definitely for salmon, as a 2lb sea trout hardly bends it.

The dual purpose 9 foot rods are all good old Hardy Jet models, just as sound and effective today as they were when I bought them thirty years ago. The No 9 is a single-handed salmon rod, excellent on small or wooded rivers, which also can be used for trailing a light bait or fly on the lough with a fixed spool reel and nylon line, making it an excellent all-rounder. The other two have caught countless fish, armed usually with a slow sinking line on the No 7, and a light floating line with its tip badly worn, making it sink, on the No 6. They are too short for good bob flywork, which is why I got my two Greys of Alnwick, long single-handers, and at this they are perfect. I have had salmon on the larger with no problems, but for its very light smaller brother a fish over 6lb might be asking a lot.

Which leaves my two veteran spinning rods, the longer an Abu which is excellent with both fixed spool and matching multiplier reels, while the old Ogden Smith early fibreglass, as it happens another great salmon killer, is at its best with heavy casting jobs, and happy when trailing a weighty lure.

To go with the above I have nine fly reels of appropriate sizes, fitted with matching lines and four spinning reels, plus a mass of flies (many my own rough efforts) and spinners, spoons, nets and other bits and pieces. I take to the lough genuinely waterproof clothing, and most importantly a tough old cushion to have in the boat. Leave it behind and you'll miss it soon enough, not least because to fish accurately and well, which is essential, you must be physically relaxed exactly as good games players, and golfers in particular, must never be tense.

These considerations cover a wide range of subjects, while the list of equipment that may be employed shows the breadth of an activity which is probably far more complex than most people realise. But in much the same way, when one compares the huge difference in environmental conditions involved between opening day for a salmon on Currane in January in a north wind and snow on the tops, with a hot July afternoon on Furnace, the contrasts and variations are equally large. Similarly in terms of purely physical difference, to believe that the techniques employed for success on a sunny June day on little Fin Lough at Delphi, are similar to those in use on mighty Melvin in a big wave, is to ignore the simple facts of geographical reality. In all these cases one has to adapt, which must mean different equipment if maximum results are to be achieved, and this in turn implies an ability to respond properly to inevitable changes in weather from time to time.

To catch brown trout effectively in variable conditions of wind and wave is not easy, sea trout are more difficult most of the time, but to persuade a salmon to take your fly in a lough is that much harder again, calling for great skills and the best equipment available.

We will next look at how to do it.

Chapter 22

Catching Fish

To persuade a salmon to take your fly fished from a boat calls for great skill. So what is this skill, and how best is it exercised on a variety of western Irish loughs?

But first a word about trolling, which is more correctly named trailing, but modern usage has it the other way. I myself, and many others, will always fish a fly for salmon and sea trout when possible, but in certain conditions the odds will very much favour a spun bait or lure against the fly, and if there is a serious demand for a fish for the table – as was once the case for my grandmother's birthday – all legal means are fair in my view. In fact I believe strongly that the reason for fishing is the practical purpose of providing food. When food is required – have no qualms about setting forth on a freezing and calm morning with the big rods out, the latest hardware thirty five yards back, all set for a serious attempt at catching a salmon. If you are just a passenger you can sit back and relax, enjoy the scenery and have a good gossip with your boatman, becoming busy only if a fish takes. On the other hand if you are on your own, managing the outboard and choosing how and where to look for a fish, things become more personal. Indeed, as once happened to me on a highland loch, I hooked two fish at once – there was half a gale blowing, I was on a rocky lee shore and it was one of those very light aluminium boats. I netted one, but lost the other, and somehow avoided shipwreck by a whisker. In such a case one is far from being a passenger, which completely changes one's feelings of achievement and what trolling is all about.

But if you are trolling please always avoid the good fly lies, unless the water is private or deserted. That said, to be effective you must cover fish, and salmon only lie in limited areas of fairly shallow water. I was told once of research on Loch Maree that showed brown trout at almost any depth, sea trout largely between twenty feet and ten feet and salmon never below twelve feet, but often just under the surface (although on my recent trip at both Melvin and Delphi they said spring salmon have been found deep down in lakes in the summer). In terms of where they would most probably be found brown trout were widely scattered, sea trout appeared to enjoy wide bays, and if shelving slowly to a sharp drop off so much the better, while salmon occupied almost exclusively rocky points and shorelines, together with sub-surface reefs, shoals and when present, sandbanks off river mouths.

Not all such salmon lies fish well when trolling and many are much better left to the fly fisherman, although I suppose that by spinning a bait from the boat – popular in North America but for me an extremely dull activity – one might have success. And here again, may I suggest you do not do this! There are few enough salmon lies where one has a chance with a fly, and these can be ruined by non-stop spinner bombardment with the greatest of ease. It is not difficult to learn how to fish a fly effectively, and the pleasure and real sense of achievement – when you get a salmon on a fly, perhaps one you tied yourself, is incomparably greater. You certainly will never forget your first!

Lastly on trolling, I have to say that I have never set out to catch sea trout by this means, or indeed by spinning in the rivers, although when after salmon I have done so. These brilliant smaller sporting fish are great takers of the fly, not least in Irish loughs, so there can be no reason for using any other means.

Now let's turn to the best bit – catching salmon and sea trout with a fly, from a boat, on these glorious Irish western waters.

This specialist branch of the fisherman's art has been the subject of only limited comment by angling writers over the years, while for Ireland we are looking at one particular doyen, head and shoulders above any others, the Dublin High Court judge, T.C. Kingsmill Moore. His book, *A Man May Fish*, is his record of someone who, while not from a fishing family, was intrigued from childhood by fish, and the best means by which one might catch them. The book, which embraces a highly readable, but remarkable, study of the Fermoyle and Costello, Connemara, fishery, which we looked at in detail earlier, is a very personal diary recording many facets of Irish game fishing, the methods employed and the environmental changes he had observed over sixty years.

It is, however, his sublime descriptions of places and people, and of the impact that natural events will have on the environment that dominates, with particular reference to fish and how to catch them. Educated at an English public school, Marlborough, and Trinity College Dublin, he was a typical product of the British Isles Edwardian intelligentsia, who fought the Germans in the first war. At the Irish Bar he rose to the top, but he never lost his ability to dig deep into the 'whys and wherefores' of the sub-surface world of his favourite game fish – the white trout. This led to his producing what now are standard fly patterns: a new 'Bumble' series of heavily palmered wet flies for use in loughs, the most famous today the 'Claret Bumble,' employed worldwide. I never met him and wish I had for, as a student – albeit much his junior – of exactly the same subjects, we would have had a lot to discuss. And here, despite his brilliantly expressed caution on laying down the law on fishing, I am certain he had developed strong views on a variety of subjects. And why wouldn't he since examining evidence in order to isolate the truth was his job? What he said on dogma was: 'No one but a master or a fool is dogmatic about fishing, and I have no pretensions to be the one nor appear the other.' But to this he added, 'Reservations continually repeated can, however, become exasperating.' Which suggests to me he felt one should never say never or always – but for goodness sake be prepared to have a view!

Against this it is extremely interesting to compare the recommendations, with regard to lough fishing, of a number of famous anglers on specific subjects. For instance how, in physical terms, to catch a salmon from a boat using a rod and line with one or more flies attached, with three basic questions:

- should the line cast be long or short?
- should the rate of retrieve be fast or slow?
- what are the differences in technique used for salmon and sea trout relative to each other?

While the answers to these questions are clearly not scientific, because the experts I am going to quote fished the same waters only occasionally, the contrasts are revealing. Thus for ordinary fishing for salmon from a boat in a lake the following makes interesting reading.

T.C. Kingsmill Moore. 'A slow and steady draw is usually most successful with white trout, while salmon prefer a more jerky motion.' He would cast up to 25 yards, and used mainly a light 10 foot rod, but was primarily after quite small white trout. He also had a 12 foot two-hander for use in gales, floods etc.

Ian Wood. The first editor of *Trout and Salmon* and a great salmon loch expert, Loch Lomond was his own special water with on one occasion seven salmon, totalling 77½lb, his best day! 'A 12 or 14 foot rod should be used so that one has sufficient rod length to work the dropper fly. There is, however, no need to fish a long line. In fact, throwing a long line is bad loch fishing. A couple of yards longer than the length of the rod is all that is necessary.' He was after salmon one hundred per cent and fished his two flies slowly just below the surface in the cold of spring, and faster with the bob well up his leader right in the surface as it got warmer. This I have always called the stroking method, and it seems he never cast a long line, or used a slow sinker. He was also an all rounder with plenty of experience on the Tay!

Arthur Oglesby. Another great all rounder if ever there was one, who was not a particularly experienced lake fisherman, but knew North Harris well. 'A quick retrieve of the flies generally brings more response from sea trout . . . ' as against slower for salmon, but not always. He liked a light line and 10 foot rod, although something longer was sometimes needed.

Hugh Falkus. In *Salmon Fishing* he says that he likes a 12 foot rod, but in fact deals with how to use it more fully in his sister publication *Sea Trout Fishing*, and makes these four significant points:

1. The strike. When a sea trout takes the fly, tighten. When a salmon takes, wait – he will hook himself.
2. Size of fly. Generally speaking larger flies should be fished for sea trout than for salmon.
3. Speed of recovery. A fly should be retrieved faster for a sea trout than for a salmon.
4. Fishing depth. As a very general rule, when fishing for sea trout concentrate on the bob fly. When after salmon concentrate on the tail fly.

Quite clear one might think but in the *Salmon* book he calls in another expert and old friend **Michael Daunt** who was his specialist adviser, as a Grimersta, Outer Hebrides, expert to describe techniques employed on that famous fishery. Daunt likes smallish tail flies, a size 10 double or small tube being typical but goes on, 'By contrast the dropper should be large: size 4 or 2. On the Grimersta the fashion is to use Elver flies . . . 1½–2 inches in length; but I think any large fly will do. Some people use a Muddler Minnow.'

Daunt also says 'In a big wind the retrieve should be relatively slow, and the flies worked right up to the boat. In a light breeze, however, in that gin-clear water, a longer line should be thrown and the flies worked faster . . . ' He is also adamant 'that, whether fast or slow the retrieve must be at an even speed. Not jerky.'

Charles McLaren. Another great loch expert and I talked to him at length about such opinions, different methods and techniques, and as the practical man he was, was adamant that the only answer was a combination of personal preference and trial and error by individuals. While he liked his long rod, light line, slow retrieve and fairly short casting method, in bad cold conditions he had found a long sinking line could be better – which was possible with a short rod, in which case a fast retrieve could produce better results.

It is with the latter flexible approach that I stand firmly, to the extent of being dogmatic! In my opinion if you are to fish a variety of differing Irish loughs to maximum effect, you have got to be a complete 'all rounder', capable of highly competent employment of a variety of fly fishing methods, and indeed trolling effectively when needs must! To achieve this having the appropriate rods, and associated equipment, is essential if you are to succeed.

I would however contribute a few points which from experience I have discovered to be important:

- when working your flies in calm conditions, you will do a lot better if they are a few inches below the surface – and for salmon I prefer only two flies
- if you are going to work the bob fly on the surface, it should be half in and half out of the water
- in shallow loughs very small lightly dressed flies, not heavy bumbles, often work well, retrieved quickly
- in big, deep loughs, and for lies close to rocks and disturbed water, big flies worked slowly are better
- the further south you go, the smaller the flies you should employ.

While it might seem correct for me now to explain in detail how this variety of methods is to be carried out physically, this would involve a specialist book on its own. There are however various publications I recommend in the Recommended Reading and if new to boat fishing, I suggest you try to study one or more. Having done so then try to get yourself into a boat with an experienced fisherman, watch his actions with care, but develop your own methods, and, above all be prepared to experiment. Not only is it sensible to be efficient at both long and short rod techniques – quick and slow retrieve – short and long line methods – that cover all eventualities, but with variety at your fingertips your confidence will grow, and it is a fact that confident anglers catch fish.

You will also discover that both salmon and sea trout will change their preferences, not only from day to day but also from hour to hour. Particularly with Connemara white trout has this been the case, where on one particular day at Costello, all they would take was a size 12 Blue Bottle fished well down with a sinking line. I only tried it in desperation, on a fine day that was a bit bright with little breeze, when most days a lightly dressed Black Pennel or Bibio would work well! The sunk fly caught twelve sea trout, the largest 2¾lb while no other fly scored once!

On what flies to use in general, I myself have real success with the sort of thing no self-respecting fishing shop would dream of selling. The well chewed appearance is a common factor, and for loughs they are all quite small and rather like hairy nymphs. That they work well in all sorts of places and conditions is certainly curious, while I have only two specific lough special recommendations:

- first that with a fall of ant, a size 10 or 12, either silver or gold, Butcher is deadly, particularly for sea trout, often in the almost flat calm conditions that go with swarming, with a long line and slow retrieve, and,
- second, that in formidable sheeting rain and a gale with black conditions of heavy cloud, as we proved on Derriana, a big heavily dressed Zulu, not smaller than size 8 with a double on the tail, will take salmon, and big sea trout, often right in the foam that builds up in the rocks of a lee shore. Do not hesitate to fish three Zulus in these conditions, but it must be a big black wave.

On which note it is important to realise that your three flies must never be allowed to show on the surface together during the retrieve, which would be entirely unnatural. For the top fly, the bob, to be cutting the surface, representing a drowning insect, certainly makes sense, so that it can be a hairy, well palmered, bumble-type fly – or a daddy long legs. The next one, the dropper, should be more a nymph in shape, or a clean bodied fly like a Butcher or Alexandra, while the tail fly should be, above all heavy, providing an anchor against which the rest of the nylon leader can be pulled tight. Thus the tail fly can often be a double hooked fly, providing exactly such a service, both during the retrieve in the water, and during casting when its weight will straighten out the leader.

With a sinking line the problems are less critical, although when casting the same position applies, and I do suggest that for salmon two flies are all you need – and certainly not four, which I have seen used.

On the generalities and opinions looked at above I would say this, that in lakes the concept of the 'induced take' applies more particularly for salmon than sea trout – most of the time. Therefore do not be afraid to work the flies really fast, although I believe at a steady, not jerky, rate.

Always fish the lightest line you can manage, from May onwards in particular, and do become expert at working the bob fly slowly right in the surface.

Short of writing that book there is little more for me to say on catching fish in loughs that could help river and reservoir fishermen. Perhaps as a postscript, if I have not made it clear already, your starting point must be a clean blackboard, a clear mind, and an ability not to have preconceived notions. Go on going to these great fisheries, and go on, like me, learning how to get better at a truly skilled means of fishing with each visit. Every cast needs to be as perfectly executed as one employed on the Test with a size 16 upstream nymph, while keeping the constant concentration that is essential while your flies are on the water, calls for the stamina of a marathon runner.

Do these things the right way, use your own imagination to develop your skills, and your reward one April day will be a couple of springers fresh from the tide, silver touched with a blush of violet borrowed from those little wild flowers on the island where we had our picnic. Do not expect big bags of salmon from loughs, although a dozen white trout to your own rod is well on the cards. But, I leave you with this thought, if the nets go, who knows?

And then as it grows on you, like the locals at Shannon airport, you too will weep when you arrive, and weep when you leave, but it's worth every inch of it!

Chapter 23

Western Lough Flies and their Use

I have mentioned that my loch fishing started back in 1946 in Scotland, at Inchnadamph, western Sutherland, under the shoulder of Ben More at the head of Loch Assynt. I had just left school and was about to go into the army, to do, it turned out, ten years serving my country. My father was our coach, and while my mother also fished, getting the largest trout we caught on Loch Gillaroo, she spent a lot of time with my brother, who being only eleven was less seriously involved. My father was remarkably patient, enthusiastic, and cast a most beautiful line singularly slowly.

Most of the time we were after loch brown trout that on balance must have averaged ½lb, with in some lochs their size only half that – very small but good fried for breakfast in hungry post-war Britain. Assynt itself had larger fish, and was famous also for its ferox, and on a visit with a friend from Sandhurst two years later, late one Saturday evening – no fishing on the Sabbath strictly observed – I had on 'Castle' beat one a fish, not a ferox, of 2¾lb. On the first visit the expert on the big loch, who fished largely the 'Head' beat where the river came in, was a Colonel Paget who most of the time used the dap with large palmered flies – my introduction to the method – which worked extremely well, his baskets of half a dozen or more trout most days, averaging over 1lb.

I can remember the flies we used in detail, in the way one often has printed in one's memory the first of many things, patterns that mostly would have been at least a hundred years old at that time. They included a lot of Teal varieties:

> Teal wing with bodies of Black, Green, Yellow, Red, and Blue and Silver
> Mallard or Grouse and Claret
> Zulu
> Alexandra
> Butcher
> Peter Ross

With these ten flies, size 10 and 12, we caught every trout we netted – the stars being Mallard/Grouse and Claret, with Teal and Green not far behind.

Today in western Ireland only four of the above would you be likely to find in an angler's box, and certainly in mine:

> Mallard and Claret
> Teal Blue and Silver
> Butcher
> Zulu

And to that for salmon and sea trout I would add:

Black Pennel	Bibio
Daddy	Green Peter
Claret Bumble	Delphi

Certainly there will be freak days when the fish will only look at some special colour or shape – including Blue Zulu, a Shrimp or a Bluebottle – but the above ten, mainly in sizes 8 to 12, with a few 6s and 14s for extreme conditions of dark and big wave, or blazing sunshine, and I would feel well supplied.

But that is by no means the whole story, for as I mentioned above the actual dressing for any one fly can vary hugely, the classic case is that of making three almost different flies from the Black Pennel.

Tied as a spider it has an entirely unpalmered smooth black body with the finest oval silver wire as a rib. Then next and very different, having a heavy seal's fur body with wide silver tinsel ribbing the hackle only at the throat and lastly almost a bumble with exactly the latter's body but with a palmered hackle along the shank from end to end, open to start with and dense at the neck. With these truly different styles I would be happy with the almost bumble on the bob, the spider in the middle, and the heavy bodied but unpalmered pattern on the tail, hook sizes for most conditions 10, 10 and 8 respectively.

But note that I said for most conditions, as to some extent whether you are mainly after salmon or sea trout will matter, although in my view the critical factor here is much more to do with how you fish the flies, as discussed above. Please also remember that this selection is for Irish lakes and not rivers where a variety of shrimp/prawn flies for salmon would be needed, plus your own old favourites – Hairy Mary, Blue Charm, Munroe Killer etc – employed in sizes for salmon by day that mainly will be larger.

This raises the point that on the lakes at Delphi a Collie Dog that is several inches long catches a lot of salmon, and on Lewis at the Grimersta elverine flies fished on the bob – all of two inches in length – have proved highly effective. Similarly when after sea trout at night big lures, often three inches or more, will take trout after trout in both sunk and floating form, with an old friend of mine the Worm Fly, in various colours, a great performer.

All one can say is that from experience it seems that when fishing loughs small flies get better results for most of us, most of the time, but – and it is a very big but – if this doesn't produce the goods be prepared to take drastic action in either direction. A huge bumble of a bob fly is almost dapping and in a gale can catch the eye of a fish – or an almost bare-hook nymph may work in a tiny ripple.

My own ideas on how flies should look owe a lot to results achieved, starting with Tony O'Sullivan on our first visit to Waterville. He was absolutely adamant that the Black Pennel was the best fly for sea trout, but it must be tied exactly the right way –

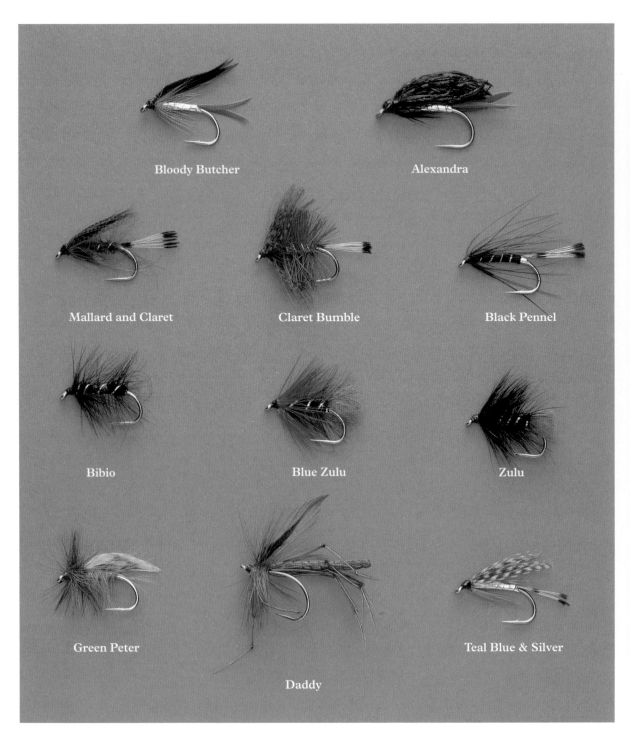

Bloody Butcher

Alexandra

Mallard and Claret

Claret Bumble

Black Pennel

Bibio

Blue Zulu

Zulu

Green Peter

Daddy

Teal Blue & Silver

Hardy's Selection

Butcher

Zulu

Black Pennel

Claret Bumble

Bibio

Peter Ross

Teal Blue & Silver

Green Peter

Daddy

Mallard & Claret

Home Made

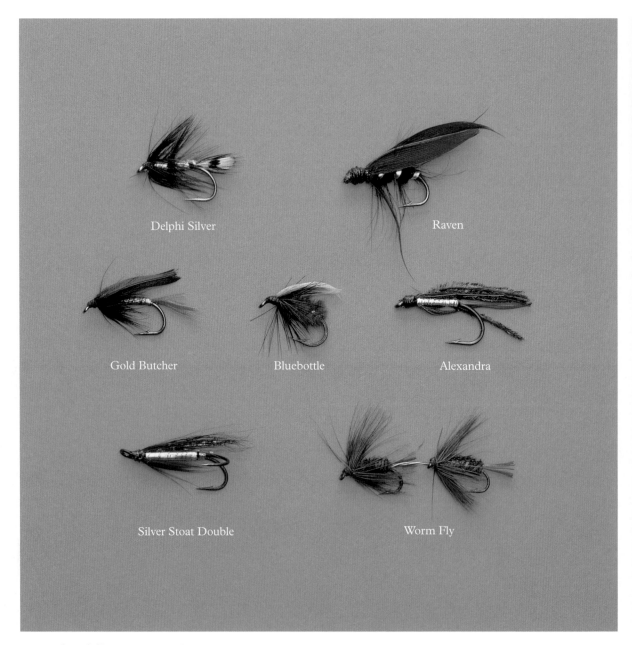

Delphi Silver

Raven

Gold Butcher

Bluebottle

Alexandra

Silver Stoat Double

Worm Fly

Lough Extras

Worm Fly (night)

Giant Sedge

Caterpillar

Shrimp

Night Lure

Sedge

Specials

good seal's fur body, well picked out, light palmer all the way, and above all the broad tinsel ribbing. Which on the face of it bears little resemblance to the Kingsmill, a fly that I don't like myself – it's too formal I suppose – although a great, well proved, catcher of white trout. But Kingsmill Moore, its inventor in his treatise on bumble patterns, being hackle versions of standard flies says that the 'Black Pennel consorts happily with the Kingsmill' just as 'the Black Zulu reproduces the character of Watson's Fancy'. Well! All I can say is up to a point – but with the first pairing both have an attractor, the jungle cock and silver tinsel respectively – and both have similar colour tails. The overall impression of black is common ground – and curiously when put in the water both seem almost to glow, an impression that increases with movement, catching the eye – that vital requirement.

I also have to admit that I do not like his bumbles either which I feel are much too rigid in construction – looking almost like a ping pong ball, and entirely unlike the Zulus I was brought up with. Then, while heavily palmered the length of the hook, at the neck the final turns of feather were the longest and tied sloping back down the shank – not sticking out at right angles. By this means the impression of a drowning moth becomes far more accurate, its concept not unlike that of a wet Mayfly, making it a credible and natural target. My own versions of bumbles are much more open and the only one I use all the time is the Claret Bumble – which seems to work just as well without the blue shoulder hackle. It catches a lot of fish, and can be deadly with brown trout on the bob in hill loughs – it once hooked six with six casts!

Much in line with that, my own varieties of the Bibio, Black Pennel and Claret Bumble – the three outstanding catchers of lough salmon and sea trout in my experience in normal conditions of wind and wave – involve somewhat similar outlines, bearing in mind that the angle of approach by most fish will be from below. That they are not in fact bumbles at all is obvious, but they do all have the common factor of a body that is made of fur and picked out, from which emerges the hackle fibres, to a greater or lesser extent. Against that bought flies always seem to be much too formal with closely wound hackles giving greater density of those fibres all the time. They may look splendid – shiny and new – able to bounce if you drop them, but to me they resemble an insect not at all, let alone an invertebrate or hatching nymph.

I have not included my new Raven fly in my list since it needs a lot more time at work to qualify. However, it has the advantage of being easy and quick to tie, and in the very limited time available to put it to work, its strike rate has been high, both in Ireland and for some big rainbows in lakes, one in Kent and another Hampshire with almost wild tough fish, and it was a Raven that the big salmon at Fin Lough went for!

To tie the Raven you need:

> Black silk and seal's fur for the body
> Silver tinsel
> Black cock hackle

With the waxed silk wind down the shank, tie in both the tinsel and, towards its thicker base, the black hackle, at the bend; dub with black seal's fur and wind to the neck; make an open palmer with the hackle up to the neck and secure; follow with the tinsel wound in the opposite direction to add strength and tie in; lay back the unused tip of the hackle down the shank as a wing; secure and varnish! There is one tricky bit, which is judging the length of hackle you will need as you tie it in to start with, but given the open palmering and fairly small flies it is quite short.

Experienced anglers will understand which of my ten flies would go where on a leader of three flies for, in general terms, heavily dressed flies will be on the bob where their ample supply of feather will make a good fuss when worked cutting the lake's surface. By the same token tail flies need to be sunk – heavier hooks, including doubles and trebles are a help – particularly in light airs. Which leaves the dropper, something that I do without when salmon are the main target, a fly which must in my view – and I repeat must – never be seen to bulge the surface during the retrieve, for two emerges in a row on exactly the same line looks to me entirely against nature, with three even worse!

All of which having been said, given a solid wind on a big lough, on a dull day – great conditions with a mild south-west air stream and a good wave – one can fish large bumbles in any position, exactly as I did on Derriana that day with the waterspouts, using two size 8 Black Zulus.

Taking my ten flies in general terms, and assuming average conditions you get this:

Bob flies Green Peter, Daddy, Claret Bumble, Zulu
Droppers Butcher, Teal Blue and Silver
Tail flies Mallard and Claret, Delphi
Universal Black Pennel, Bibio

To which I would add that both the droppers also make good tail flies, that the Delphi also works well as a dropper, and heavily dressed the Black Pennel, Bibio and Mallard and Claret are perfectly good on the bob!

One further caveat concerns a lough's dimensions as this governs the size of wave possible, with small Connemara waters unable to produce large waves, however strong the wind. In that case you may find either a slow sinking line, or heavy tail flies, can make all the difference to achieving correct presentation.

Lastly, to go with these flies, when fishing loughs in high summer with sea trout the prime target I use 7lb nylon – Maxima my normal brand – while for spring salmon I raise this to 12lb breaking strain and sometimes more. I use standard double blood knots to make the droppers, and single blood knots to attach small flies with for larger flies a double turle. And to attach the line to the leader I use a good old fashioned nylon loop – braided and special arrangements are not for me – while the nylon itself is level and in no way tapered.

All of which works, and I like the adage 'if it ain't broke – don't fix it!'

So far in this chapter I have been somewhat mean on the latter 'their use' element, which as suggested could be the subject of a book in its own right. The actual physical skills are numerous and important if flies are to be presented correctly, and safely, with high wind conditions a big factor, in which sudden gusts can blow your airborne flies dangerously off course, to threaten the eyes of your boat companions and yourself. In such, not uncommon, situations never ever cast a long line extended by false casting, not least because, having retrieved your flies, your line will be short, but all you need for a really quick long cast down wind is a fast, and high, forward throw. With the big wind behind you, given correct timing which calls for practice, you will find many yards of line projected forward, exactly as required.

In quieter conditions do not ignore the 'safety' element of this, which to the novice seems a simple task of casting from a boat. Always place him so that as he casts his line his operating arm (left handers different to right handers) is working over the bows – or stern – and not the middle of the boat. With practice you will develop the skill which allows the line to be worked immediately over your own head with safety, but it is not easy and in truly bad conditions even the experts will avoid the practice.

In which event, with the big wind to help, a roll cast with the line thrown high forward can be employed, something that works particularly well with a double handed rod, while two flies only helps avoid tangles which are inevitable in such circumstances.

I mentioned earlier my father's ability to cast his flies extremely slowly from a boat, a skill which has obvious benefits in both calm or bright conditions, for while you want your quarry to note the presence of your lures, they should look natural. That said, since salmon do not seem to be much disturbed by the arrival of large spinners being flung into a river's pool, the most clumsy presentation of even quite a large fly seems unlikely to cause panic in their minds. That sea trout are much more vulnerable is certainly the case, but your good angler will never be happy sploshing his flies on the surface of lakes or indeed of rivers.

He does want them noticed however, on which score I recently read, in Sir Alec Guinness' book, *A Positively Final Appearance*, the comment on how actors like to relate best, as they see it, to their admiring public. For without doubt, exactly as your fisherman wishes to catch his fish, so thespians must attract their audience, and I quote: 'The dark glasses for conspicuous anonymity are a Hollywood invention,' his genius with words springing from the page!

'Conspicuous anonymity' is exactly what I feel a good lough fisherman should aim to achieve with both his actions and the flies he employs. Too much being 'conspicuous' will put the fish off, and too much 'anonymity' will leave you unobserved and equally fishless! While tailored to match the conditions of the day, it is therefore up to the person presenting his flies to get the right compromise. It's always up to you!

Chapter 24

Competitions

At the very start of my 2001 visit to Ireland to complete the research required for this book I went, at the suggestion of The Irish Tourist Board, to have a look at the World Wet-Fly Angling Championships on Lough Mask, a fishery that, being landlocked, could hardly be included as part of a treatise on salmon and sea trout in the ordinary way. However, I knew something about the event from reading the late David Street's beautiful book *Fishing in Wild Places*, for Mask at one point had been a regular holiday destination for him and his long term fishing companion Bill Storer. In fact the latter, a Westmorland migrant to Dublin where as an accountant he had settled, had at one point taken a summer off, between jobs to become a professional boatman on Mask which he therefore knew in great detail.

The start – slow ahead

An aquatic cavalry charge

The two of them would pitch a tent on the lake's shore, fish by day with both wet flies and the dap, sell any surplus trout to the hotel, and support the modest night life of their local town, Ballinrobe. He became a staunch champion of the lough, which is ten miles long and 20,000 acres, being wide open to the sky, for while the Patry Mountains are there to the west, with the hills of Joyce's country to their south to remind you that the wilds of Connemara and southern Mayo are not far off, there are no cliffs of black rock leaning over the shore to threaten the harmless interloper. This is in style much closer to Ireland's famous central lakes, Sheelin, Owel or Ennell than Corrib, and the solid limestone base provides an almost unlimited food supply. And that means strong, large trout, their outward colour rather paler and less golden than sometimes is the case, being pink fleshed and perfect for the table. The large number I saw weighed-in ranged from about 1¼lb to 4¼lb, to which ferox can be added by trolling enthusiasts, with fish up towards 20lb being regularly netted.

Mask is no place for the casual visitor to be messing about in a boat for, due to the limestone, numerous sharp and dangerous rocks and reefs exist, often well out from the shore, capable of splitting the hull of a fast moving boat apart with the greatest ease. Caution is therefore essential, exactly as is the case on Corrib and indeed all limestone lakes, and as we saw on Conn the marking of these hazards is no bad idea.

The competition, start point Cushlough Bay on the east shore, was beginning on 2 August, with four qualifying days, followed by the final on Bank Holiday 6 August, and I arrived in time to see some of the fourth day's afternoon activity, together with the whole of the final day. About 120 boats with two rods per boat and a boatman took part and I observed the start from the starter's boat itself, a sight not to be forgotten! For this involved what I can only describe as an aquatic cavalry charge, as the fifty leading boats – starting slowly from the shore but accelerating progressively – having the largest engines and capable of considerable speed, set themselves roughly in line abreast immediately behind the starter who was heading out of the bay into open water. Once there, when clear of land, the signal to go was given via a blast on a hooter! That the discipline which control of

One in the net in mid-lough

Time to get going

such a conglomeration of small boats requires – all obliged to keep behind the starter until the hooter went – was well below the best traditions of Dartmouth may well be imagined, boats on the flanks edging improperly ahead, while those more central to the advance became increasingly tightly packed, bumping each other with seemingly little effect, strangely producing no shouts of 'water' or signs of anxiety! This is not a pastime for those of a nervous disposition, and I was glad I had been brought up in boats!

I'm not a good reporter so the exact detail of all this I failed to record but I think the timing was a 10.00 am start with a 5.00 pm finish, most boats that I saw stopping for a breather and picnic on an island at midday. There was a strong south-westerly wind with high cloud and a rather 'hard' feeling – but it was August – and not the best time of year to fill a basket.

The winner caught four fish, average weight about 3lb, all taken late in the day, and not far from the launch point at that, which made me wonder why almost the entire fleet had headed for the other side of the lough for starters. This was some four miles away so that there and back must mean at least an hour of fishing lost!

While we all know only too well that in things physical 'handsome is as handsome does', I was astonished at some of the antics those who were fishing employed. To start with when fishing from a boat to employ a hugely long line is by no means an advantage – which it can be when fishing from the bank – as since this means a lot of false casting to get the line out, much time is wasted. And that means, for the flies are in the air and not in the water, less time for a fish to see what is on offer, and to grab it. Only if using a deep sinking line is length a clear help otherwise, with some assistance from a following breeze, lift off and cast immediately must be correct and indeed with practice, easy to manage!

Mask's annual event clearly is a big social and important angling occasion, the prizes being of considerable value – including two brand new 17 foot lough boats – and an outboard or two! I expect also that to do well may be of commercial value – so-and-so the winner used a particular reel, rod, line etc. – but I forgot to ask, and I hope this is not a big factor. Which raises the question 'why take part anyway?' or indeed 'if it's not commercial what is the motive?' To which the obvious retort must be 'to win', and that introduces an entirely different set of factors to the debate, and to start with 'why do you want to win', or 'who do you want to beat', etc. Fishing is not golf, or racing a horse, or playing tennis, as its *raison d'être* is the logical and sensible pursuit of food! And therefore game fishing is not the same as coarse fishing where the catch is not consumed, there being no point in keeping the fish. Just like shooting for the pot the skilled operator will come home with more fish than the novice, so to fish well is important. To prove you are better than others at this can be interesting and a help to those who are learning but for me fishing will never be a competition! However here I should declare an interest, since I have indeed, myself, once by mistake taken part in a competition, and won it – or rather my fishing companion, son Julyan, won it – back in 1974 at Waterville.

Each year in August, during their festival week, on Lough Currane they hold an anglers' competition which was news to us – a two day event, on a boat against boat basis, two rods per boat, your boatman an observer. Vincent O'Sullivan was running it, and we only discovered we were taking part the day before, in fact I had never heard of any form of Currane competition before! But, staying as we were at the Butler Arms, there seemed no good reason not to take part since we would only do precisely what we meant to do anyway – with Paddy our boatman – go fishing on Currane!

It was a glorious August spell and, while the lake was full of fish, on day one without a cloud in the sky and not a breath of wind, the conditions were hardly encouraging. But we worked hard when a little breeze got up at lunchtime, so that with four sea trout making around 5lb, that evening we were in fourth position. Brod O' Sullivan was leading, and was the only person to have a decent trout in his bag, it being 4¼lb, to add to several small ones.

Day two was exactly the same, the lake a mirror with absolutely clear sky as we

The largest – 4¼lb.

headed to the top end of the lake, the fish we had caught the previous day mainly around Tern Island, at that time before the mink came, full of nesting Arctic Terns. And in the calm, about two hundred yards to the south-west of the island we saw several times a large fish – probably a salmon and certainly not one of those little grilse – jump clear of the lough, returning with a considerable splosh, always in the same place.

By 11.30 there was still no wind but if the weather followed the same pattern, with the land mass heating up inland, by about 1 o'clock an on-shore breeze would get up, so why not I suggested have an early lunch and be all set to go as soon as we had some ripple on the surface. This as they say with winning tactics at bridge was to prove the 'key play', for just as that breeze got going to a fishable strength, there we were on station south-west of Tern Island, all set to drift down right over our jumping friend's nose. And I thought as we eased towards his lie, dear God a blessing for this one please – and I swear this is true – promptly changed my prayer to give Julyan the benefit, for next day he was leaving.

Two minutes later Julyan hooked a fish, and I thought that in my life perhaps I might have missed out a bit on the power of prayer. However the fish did not do anything much.

'It's something solid', came from the bows.

Then a pause followed by Paddy.

'I don't think it's very big.'

Whereupon the insulted creature leapt high out of the water, a thick heavy fish of great power and probably a salmon, something we debated at some length, our views changing as we saw a lot more of him. For eight times he jumped high for us to inspect, with Paddy the first to say, without doubt, a big sea trout! And he was right, as three-quarters of an hour later, in the net we could confirm just that!

Time for lunch

Julyan had an 8ft 6in Hardy Jet fibreglass rod – nylon of 7lb breaking strain – a good dressed silk line on an old Hardy Perfect reel with ample backing. And it went well to start with as the fish ran about the lake, taking line and being worked back, Paddy at the oars helping. But, and a huge but, what do you do when a fish like that sulks – in this case lies almost under the boat 15 feet below one, for he could bend the rod double and nothing happened. The answer it turned out was to pull at an angle, by moving the boat away, rather than from immediately above – although nothing dramatic occurred in that case either. But terribly slowly the fish tired, and even more slowly he came to the surface from time to time, so that in the end he was netable, although still far from played out.

The knots had held, the hook remained in place, and the truly ancient Alexandra which had been my father's – size 12 with minimal dressing – had won the day, the middle dropper of his three fly cast. It was the only time we had either of us tried it, and I think the only time I ever saw a white trout in Ireland take one, Julyan's comment, having chosen it, that he thought 'it looked rather good'.

The best bag 7¼lb

Finals day is popular

His trout weighed one ounce under 8lb, and nobody could remember as large a sea trout being taken on a fly from the lake, although since then, with the traps off, larger fish are sometimes caught. To add to this, that afternoon, I managed to land another four small ones exactly similar to our previous day's effort – Julyan resting on his laurels. One curiosity in this was that one of the four came at my bob fly a total of five times before making contact – absolutely fresh from the sea he was in no way put off by missing four times – a determined loser if ever there was!

A large silver bowl was presented to us, for the big fish had made us very clear winners of the competition – greatest overall weight, largest sea trout, no salmon caught. And by tradition the bowl was kept topped up by the winners, largely with Guinness, to keep the party going late into the night – a not inexpensive privilege in itself. But for someone forbidden alcohol post-jaundice – my personal position at that time – I had to wonder, in cold sobriety, whether winning a competition was such a good idea after all!

Envoi

Having started on this tale of a fisherman's wanderings at Waterville, I seem to have finished up back exactly there as I reel in the line and hang up my rod. That I have enjoyed this exercise, which has meant recalling such fun and enjoyment in so many often spectacular places, with so many pleasant people contributing so much, is a fact and surely not surprising. If thereby this simple book can encourage others to follow in my footsteps, absorbing the findings of Kingsmill Moore while taking the advice of Peter O'Reilly, with a constructive and personal approach they will find great and continuing interest in a pastime that is as old as mankind.

Fishing a fly well calls for considerable physical skill, concentration, and imagination, so that always the angler faces a challenge, which over the years becomes condensed into a few seconds – that truly great moment a fish takes your fly. While the struggle thereafter may be hair-raising and full of heart stopping moments is certainly true, and your physical performance must be faultless. But a physical performance is precisely what playing a fish is, while to get such a fish to take your fly in the first place is the difficult bit, and if you can manage to do that using flies you have made yourself you will feel even better, for that is the triumph!

You can fish into great old age, and continue to improve your skills as your knowledge steadily grows, as I can demonstrate with sixty-seven years trout fishing and fifty-five years on lakes behind me. The fly patterns I use, often with real success, are today nearly all my own inventions, while the joy that comes with modern rod technology makes the use of today's rods an incomparable pleasure – although I still prefer my old Perfect reels.

If mankind can now reverse the trend of falling salmon and sea trout numbers, which given our rivers are today so much cleaner should be possible, the outlook for us anglers who love the wilds, with their wild fish that come from the ocean, will be transformed. And to that end I have committed myself with trials of a new salmon rearing system – the first smolts now at sea – 'The Twin Lake Method' taking place in Cornwall. Wish us luck – and watch this space!

Lough Acoose – top of the Caragh

Appendix

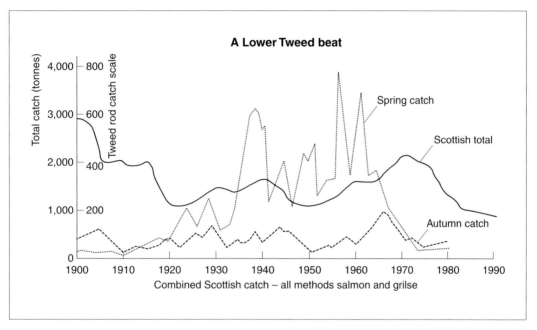

Scottish Catch 1900-1990

Recommended Reading

There are only a tiny handful of books on lake fishing for salmon and sea trout, some of which were published many years ago, including these.

Sea Trout Fishing, Hugh Falkus, Cassell Illustrated, 2002.
Salmon Fishing, Hugh Falkus, Cassell Illustrated, 2002.
A Man May Fish, T.C. Kingsmill Moore, Colin Smythe, 1979.
Art of Sea Trout Fishing, Charles McLaren, Oliver and Boyd, 1963.
Trout and Salmon Loughs of Ireland, Peter O'Reilly, Collins Willow, 1992.
Trout and Salmon Rivers of Ireland, Peter O'Reilly.
Fishing in Wild Places, David Street, The Golden Grove Book Co. Ltd., 1989.
My Way with Salmon, Ian Wood, George Allen and Unwin, 1957.

Index

Aasleagh Falls 99, 110
Achill Island 115
Acoose, Lough 37, 38, 40
Arrow, Lough 147
Ashford Castle Hotel 93
Ballynahinch Castle Hotel 53, 54, 55, 99
Ballynahinch,
    Loughs 56, 60
    River 147
Ballysodare River 147
Bangor Erris 131, 137
Barrett, Walter 16
Beltra, Lough 12, 97, 112, 117, 118, 119,126
Black River 93
Black River (Killarney) 44
Bonet, River 148
Bradley, Terence 155
Bundorragha River 100, 107
Burrishoole 12, 97, 107, 122
Butler Arms Hotel 12, 17
Butlers Pool 12, 17, 25

Capal, Lough 28
Capal Stream 17. 18
Caragh, Lough 37, 38
Caragh System 34, 35
Carra, Lough 87, 94, 97
Carrickillawallia, Lough 74
Carrarevagh Hotel 93
Careysville 85
Carrowmore, Lough 117, 126, 129, 131
Carrowniskey River 115
Cashel River 71
Chaplin, Charlie 23

Claire, River 90
Clew Bay 113
Clifden 53
Clonadoon 73
Cloon, Lough 37, 38
Cloonaghlin, Lough 28, 30
Clougher, Lough 74, 77
Colman, Bishop 114
Colyagh, Lough 149
Cong 53, 87, 94
Conn, Lough 85, 97, 118, 139, 141
Connaught 51
Connemara 51
Corchoran, Tom 31
Cornamona, River 93
Corrib, Lough 85, 86, 87 et seq
Cosgrove, Evelyn 137
Cosgrove, John 132
Cosgrove, Kenneth 129, 132
Costello and Fermoyle 65, 70, 71
Costello, Frank 94, 95
Croagh Patrick 113, 117, 130
Cross, River 139
Cullin, Lough 139
Cummeenduff Lakes 47, 49
Cummeragh River 13, 18, 27, 28, 60
Currane, Lough 11, 15, 33

Dawcross, River 52
Deel, River 142
Delphi, 32, 53, 97, 98, 107, 126
Dereen, Lough 60, 73
Derriana, Lough 29, 30, 31, 32, 37, 60
Derryclare, Lough 56, 57

Doo Lough 32, 101, 106
Drowse River 144, 154, 156
Drumcliffe River 151

Enniscoe House 143
Equipment needed 165, 166
Erriff, River 53, 97, 111, 126

Feagh, Lough
Fermoyle Estate 65
Fermoyle Lodge 76
Fermoyle, Lough 73
Fin Lough 103, 104, 108
Fitzjohn, Geoffrey 77
Flesk, River 43, 48
Furnace, Lough 117, 123, 126
Flies 174-182
    Bibio 28, 60, 71, 123, 126, 135
    Beltra Badger 120
    Black Pennel 20, 22, 23, 24, 28, 60,
        71, 104, 126, 131, 135
    Black Goldfinch 82
    Black Zulu 32
    Claret Bumble 104, 106, 126, 131
    Collie Dog 106
    Daddy Longlegs 22, 106, 109
    Delphi Silver 106
    Gary Dog 82
    Gold Butcher 71
    Green Highlander 82
    Green Peter 109, 126, 131, 132, 137
    Hairy Mary 20, 106, 120
    Kenyaman 126
    Kingsmill 162
    Munroe Killer 82
    Peter Ross 28, 106
    Shrimp 131
    Silver Doctor 120
    Silver Stoat 20, 104, 106, 109

Thunder and Lightning 120
Tosh 82
    Watson's Fancy 104
    Willie Gunn 82
    Zulu 32, 106, 126, 135

Gallagher, Terry 76
Galway 51
Galway Fishery 81
Galway Weir 80, 84
Garavogue River 148
Garrison 155
Gaythorne Hardy, A E 15
Gill, Lough 147
Gillaroo trout 156
Glencar, Lough 147, 149
Glencar Hotel 35, 36, 37, 41
Glencullin, Lough 101, 105, 108
Glenicmurrin, Lough 71, 72, 75
Glenisland Co-operative 119
Gowla 65, 66, 67
Guinness, Arthur 125

Huggard, Noel 17, 43, 57

Inagh, Lough 56, 57, 60, 63
Inagh, Lough Lodge Hotel 63
Inny, River 16, 35
Inverbeg 65, 68
Invermore 65, 68
Iskanamacteery, Lough 30

Jamsie 90
Joyces Country 53
Joyce's River 87, 95, 96

Kelly, Grace 117
Kerry, County 11
Killary Harbour 53, 99

Killarney Lakes 42, 46
Killimer 51
Kingsmill Moore, Judge T C 71, 72, 89, 100, 135
Kylemore Abbey 50
Kylemore Loughs 53

Lanne, River 43, 47, 49
Leane, Lough 42, 43, 46
Lobster Bar, Waterville 25, 27
Louisburgh 115

Mackcross, Lough 47
Mamm Cross 91
Mantle, Peter 10, 101, 103
Martin, Richard 55
Mask, Lough 87, 94, 97
Mayo, County 53
McLaren, Charles 145
Melvin, Lough 144, 145, 154, 158
Middle Lake, Killarney 47
Moy, River 85, 97, 138, 140
Muckanagh, Lough 73
Mumford-Smith family 117

Namona, Lough 28, 30, 60
Netting catch 13
Newport 11, 97, 113
Newport River 115, 116
Newport House Hotel 113, 116, 119
Nixon, Sean 127
North West Fishery Board 139

O'Malley, Grace 55
Oorid, Lough 61
O'Reilly, Peter 125, 126
O'Riordan, Ted 43
O'Sullivan
  Brod 17

Jack 20
  Michael 25
  Tony 12, 21
  Vincent 19, 25
Oughterard 87, 91, 93
Owenmore, River 129, 137
Owenduff, River 130
Owenriff, River 91

Pontoon Bridge 142

Reagh, Lough 37
Roberts, Charles 123
Rossinver 155
Rusheen, Lough 71, 73

St Patrick 87
Salmon Research Agency 125, 127
School House Loughs 65
Screeb system 65, 68
Seagrave, Barry 143
Shanawona, Lough 65, 75
Sligo, 2nd Marquess of 100
Spiddal system 65, 68

Tarbert 51
Tawnyard Lough 99, 111, 113
Thompson, Kieran 116, 121
Tourist Board, Irish 57
Tralee 51
Tweed Salmon records 85

Upper Lake, Killarney 47

Waterville 11, 97
Western Region Fishery Board 81

Zetland Hotel 66